First Published 2019 (eBook)
This edition was published in January 2023
ISBN: 9781838320317

Whilst every care has been taken to ensure the accuracy of the information in this book, the passage of time will always bring changes. The author and publisher cannot accept responsibility for errors that may occur, nor shall we be held liable for any loss, damage or accidents incurred whilst following the guidance in this book.
If you have any problems or questions, please email support@wandering-bird.com

Cover image: Verdon Gorge, France
See more at **www.wandering-bird.com**

An unexpected twist

When I first had the **crazy idea** to quit my job as an air traffic controller so we could tour Europe long term, we had many worries about **what could go wrong**.

We spent hours discussing all the various disasters which could befall us, including health and financial concerns, and how we might be able to plan or avoid these potential pitfalls should they happen.

Never, not once, did we discuss what to do if there was a **deadly virus which causes a global pandemic** and all the borders closed.

We never imagined there would be a time where we were **trapped on the wrong side of a border** and couldn't return to visit relatives when we needed to or when we would have to console our sobbing daughter over Face-time because she was stuck on her own and scared out of her mind.

Travel has changed dramatically since early 2020 and, although borders have re-opened and people are moving again, the way people feel comfortable about travelling has changed. Even now, fully vaccinated and with precautions in place, my husband is not entirely happy getting on a plane; something he's done at least once a month for years.

Many people are turning to motorhomes and campervans as a way of travelling whilst still maintaining a small bubble. More and more people are discovering the freedom of being able to travel overland to explore new places, whilst sleeping in your own bed and having your own kitchen and bathroom with you.

People are also reluctant to plan big overseas trips in advance, in case things change and borders close again. One of the huge advantages of being able to travel with a motorhome, is that you can adapt your plans very quickly *(this is also true if you happen to have bad weather or noisy neighbours on the campsite!)*

It's impossible to predict the future, or how the full effect of COVID-19 might impact travel in years to come. The rules are also changing regularly, so **I haven't included much about them in this guide** as I don't want it to be misleading. **Please check & follow the government guidelines before travelling.**

I think 2020 also brought into focus how unpredictable life is. The number of people buying motorhomes and campervans has increased dramatically, as people look to enjoy life now, rather than waiting until retirement to get a van and see the world.

Setting off for a foreign country takes a certain amount of courage. There's something magical about seeing another van from your home country when you're somewhere new; a camaraderie felt that we're 'all in this together'. I think that's become even more true in recent years and a bond is formed when you chat to fellow motorhomers on a site far from home, or even just wave to one as it passes by.

We have started travelling again as much as possible; as I write this, I'm on a fantastic campsite on the SW coast of France, just down from Biarritz, with incredible views of the ocean. There are at least 2 other British vans on site, plus Dutch, German, Spanish and of course French. Whatever our story or origin, we're all here, living the dream.

It doesn't matter whether you are brand new to motorhoming, returning to van-life after pursuing other interests or are an old hand with many miles under your wheels; it doesn't matter whether you're only planning the 'odd weekend' away or want to change your life completely and live in a van full-time, or whether you prefer campsites or aires or staying off-grid.

The point is that you are DOING it. Taking every opportunity to squeeze the most out of each day and seeing as much as you can see.

I hope you find this guide a useful addition to your European travels and may I take this opportunity to wish you and yours the very best of health & happiness. I hope you have some amazing adventures.
If you're on Instagram, feel free to tag me, I'd love to see where you go. You can find and follow us at:

@wanderingbird.adventures

Safe travels and I can't wait to see where you end up!

Kat x

Table of Contents

Introduction

Broadly speaking, there are two types of people.
The first is the type who will get into their motorhome with **only their phone, wallet and a ticket** to cross the Channel, and merrily head off to Europe with little to no planning, ready to 'see where the road takes them.'
That's my husband, through and through *(and if you glanced at this book and thought* ***'pfft, what's the big deal about going to Europe'****, then it's probably you too!)*
And then there are the rest of us. We're the ones who like to plan or want to know a TEENY bit more about what we might find in Europe- especially if we don't speak the language(s).
We worry about things like:

- How do we find somewhere to stay?
- How do we get gas?
- Where do we find fresh water or empty waste?
- What are the laws?
- Which route should we take?
- How do I drive my motorhome on the 'wrong' side of the road?
- Heck, will my motorhome even fit in a cute French village or up a mountain road?

The list of questions goes on (and on... and on) and the whole thing can end up feeling completely intimidating.

I get it. I felt exactly the same before our first trip to Europe.
We headed over the Channel with the grand total of **15 days motorhoming experience.** Ever.

It's safe to say we were out of our comfort zone and had no clue what we were doing. And it didn't go well...
In fact, we had **one of the worst motorhoming trips we've ever had,** which included mistakes like:

- Heading to the Italian Lakes… in August (DON'T do this- far too many people and very few parking spots!)
- Trying to wild camp around the Italian lakes (again… big mistake).
- Realising our brakes hadn't been serviced properly and losing them completely as we were driving down a BIG mountain in the Alps… (Yes, this was TERRIFYING.)
- Trying to figure out how to pre-book an aire (you can't).

and a million more other tiny things which went wrong because we had no clue what we were doing.

That trip could have been **the end of our motorhoming life**, except for one tiny thing… we LOVED it. *(Except the brakes failing part- that was not fun.)*
But we learnt so much and spent great times together as a family. We discovered that we could move or change our plans if we weren't having fun or if the neighbours were too noisy.

We also learnt that if (and when!) things did go wrong, we could DEAL with them. Even in a foreign country where we don't speak the language.

One of the most frustrating things about motorhoming is how hard it is to learn what you need to know. You spend all this money on a van... and then you're left to figure the rest out on your own.

Sure, there are online forums and Facebook groups if you're brave enough *(more info on ours which is dedicated to beginners can be found in 'Pre-trip Planning)* but it's so difficult to get sensible answers to basic questions.
Worse, when you turn up at a campsite, everyone else seems to have it 'all figured out' and you feel stupid, not to mention that when you do make a mistake (and you will!) it damages your already shaky confidence.
All in all, it's a wonder any of us ever go anywhere!
The main reason I started my website and Youtube channel (Wandering Bird) was partly to share our adventures, but also to share the mistakes we made and things we learnt. I knew that if we felt unsure and underconfident, others would benefit from our knowledge.

Since we started touring, we've visited plenty of countries across Europe. We've been to a lot of places, made a lot of mistakes and learnt a lot of lessons.
We've dealt with a poorly dog, fire in our motorhome, getting horrendously lost (with no phone signal), running

out of gas (without the right connectors), having to reverse three miles up a hill (with a trailer) because we went down the wrong road and **running out of Jaffa Cakes**! All in all, it's been dramatic.

We now feel fairly confident that we could go anywhere and deal with any situation. And that's what I want to share with you here, everything we've learned and the mistakes we've made, so you can avoid making them too.

Getting the most from this guide & QR codes

I don't want this guide to be something which you flick through, then put away on a shelf. I want it to be a helpful companion, well-thumbed and scribbled in the margins.

This book started as a digital PDF guide, with plenty of links to helpful resources and additional information. Obviously, in printed form that's much harder, but I've included QR codes throughout when I think you'll find them useful.

To use these, all you need to do is point the camera of your smart phone at the code box, and it will bring up a weblink (usually to a page on the Wandering Bird website.) There, you'll find resources and other info to help you further.
We've made the size of this printed book small, so you can tuck it easily into a pocket or cupboard on the van, ready for whenever you need it.

I also don't want you to feel overwhelmed, we did NOT wake up one day just knowing all this stuff. It's been built up over years of travelling almost full-time.

Nothing can beat the confidence that first-hand experience on the road brings but, until you get out there and do it yourself, I hope this guide prepares you in every possible way.

As you'll see next, taking our motorhome to Europe changed our lives. Let's see if we can change yours too.

Owner of www.wandering-bird.com

Our Story

We never meant to buy a motorhome.

We certainly never meant to change our lives, for me to quit my career and for us to live almost full-time in a motorhome for several years.

After all, REAL people didn't do that... right?

Before I get ahead of myself, let's start at the beginning.

If we've not met before: Hi, I'm Kat. My husband and I have always been a bit 'weird'. We lived on boats for 15 years; partly to save money and partly because we loved the view! We've never been excited about big houses in the suburbs and didn't want to pay off a mortgage for the next 30 years.

Instead, we lived small on boats and spent our money travelling. We got married in Victoria Falls in Zambia, we honeymooned with the elephants in Botswana, we've marvelled at the Northern lights in both Norway and Iceland, we almost ran out of fuel in the middle of Mexico (surrounded by drug cartels) and we've eaten ourselves into a pancake coma in America. **Twice.**
We love to travel and explore new places and we both get itchy feet if we don't have the next adventure booked. But we've always worked, and travel needed to fit around our jobs and our daughter's schooling. We didn't think there was any other way.

Yet, despite the love of travel, we always dismissed the idea of buying a motorhome or campervan. After all, we already had a boat and motorbikes- why did we need ANOTHER form of transport?

Then, in 2017, our lives changed dramatically. We lost my mother-in-law, who was one of the world's 'good people'. Her passing was swift and unexpected, and really shook us out of our rut.

To try to cheer my poor husband up, I took him to the local Triumph motorcycle dealership; he'd always wanted a touring / adventure bike and I thought going to look at them might make him smile.

Turns out, 'going to look' led to us buying not just one, but TWO Triumph Scrambler motorbikes, and us booking a trip to France to take them on an adventure.
We towed them down to southern France on a trailer behind the car and started to explore. It was a great trip, but we had a lot of trouble finding suitable places to stay overnight.
We were travelling with our teenage daughter (who is NOT a fan of camping) but many places either didn't like the fact that we had motorbikes or were not the sort of place we wanted to stay overnight with our daughter. It was a tough balance.
Until one day, riding near Bordeaux, we saw a motorhome pulling two motorbikes on a trailer. Immediately, we knew we'd found our solution. If we

bought a van, we could go wherever we liked, save money on hotel rooms (our daughter was old enough to need her own) and take the bikes to explore. It was the perfect solution.
So, the very next week, with almost no research and very little clue what we were doing, we bought the first motorhome to fit our requirements, which were:

- Could sleep three of us in two separate areas.
- Had a dinette big enough for 3.
- Had the ability to tow a trailer.
- Was within our (not very large) budget.

That was how we found 'Little Ship', a McLouis Tandy. Unsurprisingly, this motorhome was wrong for us in almost every way!
(If you haven't yet bought your van and want some guidance to help you make a better choice, visit ***wandering-bird.com/buy*** *for help.)*
A week later, we'd emptied half our kitchen into the van (because we knew nothing about payload) and we set off for a long weekend in southern Wales. It was magical.

Two weeks after that, we spent 10 days in Scotland, where we discovered wild van camping for the first time. *(We also discovered midges, and rain like we'd never seen it before…)*

Our first motorhome 'Little Ship' in Switzerland

And then, with the grand total of 15 days of motorhoming experience, we set off into Europe. To the Italian Lakes. In the middle of August.

We hadn't booked any campsites, because we thought we could wild camp (spoiler, you can't around the Italian Lakes, especially in Summer), we didn't understand how aires worked (I spent hours trying to figure out how to find them and book them; you can't) and we didn't have most of the gear we legally needed to carry... because we didn't know we should have been carrying it.

Looking back now, I cringe; we were so woefully unprepared. BUT (and here's the most important thing), we survived. Heck, not only did we survive, we LOVED it. Yes, some parts were less than fun, such as the brake failure in the Alps and the trouble we had finding somewhere to stay overnight around the Italian Lakes (more on those later), but there were so many highlights too.

One of the most memorable moments was finding ourselves wild camping in the Swiss Alps at the top of a mountain.

It was the exact same day as when our brakes had just failed; we'd had them replaced by a local garage and we paused at the top of the next mountain to build courage before going down the other side again.
Whilst we were here, we realised that vans were staying overnight so we decided to do the same.

We made dinner, then went to sit outside with a hot chocolate... and looked up to see the Milky Way shining down on us. **The ACTUAL Milky Way,** in all its breath-taking glory. I'd never seen it before in real life; not like that.

I was mesmerised. I remember turning to my husband in awe and asking what we needed to change in our lives in order to see this again. What other amazing things existed in the world which we hadn't seen yet? How did we get more time to explore and have adventures?

(Our photography skills are lacking, but I promise it's there!)

THAT is the moment which changed our entire lives. I wanted to stay up there another few nights to see it again. But, instead, we had to return home. To work. To "real life" with all its rushing around and barely seeing each other. And I didn't want to go.

That night under the stars, we realised we wanted **adventure and freedom now**, whilst we were still young enough to enjoy it. What started as a fun, fly-away comment took root and began to grow into a wonderfully crazy idea (my favourite kind!)

The whole way back to the UK, we discussed what was keeping us in one place and how we could change it. My job was the biggest reason we couldn't travel as much as we wanted to; Mr WB could do a lot of his work from the road but they tend to like air traffic controllers actually being on location!

I started researching simple living, early retirement and living in a van long-term. I began to envision a life beyond what we had; one which allowed us time to enjoy the simpler things in life.

After looking at our bank accounts for days, figuring out how much we needed to live on, where we could save money and how we might downsize to only one income, I applied for a year-long sabbatical from my job. We wanted a year to go off and have adventures.

However, as soon as we started saving and downsizing, we quickly realised that, if we drastically changed our lifestyle and reduced our bills, we could afford for me not to go back to work. At all. We could live and travel entirely on my husband's wage.
I'll be honest, this was one of the hardest decisions of my life. I was only 35: **did I really want to walk away from a career I'd worked so hard for?** I struggled to make such a huge decision but, in the end, it came down to a quote by Robin Sharma:

"Don't live the same year 75 times and call it a life"

Without realising, this was exactly what we had been doing. Life had become 'routine' and we'd become sucked into the rat race. Every year was the same battle to get school holidays off, or time off at Christmas and cram as much into those short breaks as possible.

I handed in my notice the very next day.

We were adamant we wanted to explore and have adventures whilst we still could, for as long as we could. If we needed to stop travelling and work in the future, we could do that. **But if we didn't change, nothing else would.**

Whilst we still had two incomes, we upgraded our motorhome and gear (to a Swift 496), then got rid of the majority of our 'stuff', reduced our bills as much as possible and started planning our travels.
I left work in March 2018 and our first big trip was to Norway. We spent 5 weeks travelling up and back and we LOVED it (although sadly it rained pretty much every day).

Since then, we've explored 17+ countries and travelled over 60,000 miles. We've watched the sun rise over Stonehenge, walked behind waterfalls, seen the Disney Castle and paid our respects at the Menin Gate in Belgium. But our true love is still the mountains- there's something about them which speaks to our souls.

We travelled with & home-schooled our daughter Jade for just over a year.

Jade and I on a suspension bridge in Switzerland

Now, she's grown up and is in university, but does still travel with us occasionally. We've also downsized the van (to a Swift 685 Escape) and adopted a cocker spaniel called Mac. He LOVES travelling in the van & exploring each new place.

Mr WB, Mac and me in the Dolomites, Italy

Of course, 2020 put a damper on proceedings. We found ourselves locked down in France and ended up renovating a small house, just so we had somewhere to park the motorhome and stay safe.
Now that borders have opened up again, we're travelling as much as possible, but it's a balance between needing to be back in the UK for a while so Mr WB can visit clients and ensure his business survives this crazy time.
On the upside, not travelling so much gave me time to sit down and write this guide for you! So, that's our story.

Let's get on with helping you have your own epic adventures!

Pre-trip planning

As you might already have realised, I am a recovering planner. I try my hardest not to dictate every teeny tiny aspect of a trip (there was one memorable time I scheduled in coffee and lunch breaks to the exact minute- Mr WB was not impressed!) Instead, I've learnt to 'go with the flow' on an actual trip… as much as possible!

BUT (and this is important), the reason I'm able to do that is because I know we are (mostly) prepared.
I know our kit is packed and ready. I know we've got food and water onboard. I know our paperwork is in order.

In order to have the freedom to enjoy a trip, I believe it's essential to do some planning before you go. It will definitely be better for your wallet if you want to avoid the fines.
So, work your way through this section and I'll see you on the other side.

Don't forget, if you have questions, you can join our **Wandering Bird Facebook group using the QR code here.** iIt's a great place for beginners or more experienced travellers alike to ask questions, share destinations and compare notes.

Choosing Where to Go

Ok, let's start with the fun bit: planning your itinerary for your trip to Europe.

But where should you go? Believe it or not, I get asked this question a LOT. Deciding where to go is sometimes the hardest bit, especially if you've never been to Europe before. There are so many options.

Here is a little questionnaire to help you figure out where to start your planning:

- Are you happy to go to a foreign country? Driving on the wrong side of the road, speaking a foreign language, eating foreign foods? Not everyone is, and that's ok. Better to figure that out now, rather than later!
- How long do you have for your trip? A weekend, week, more?
- How long do you want to drive for each day?
- Are you happy to drive on motorways/ toll roads (i.e. you can go further, faster) or do you only want to drive on smaller, free roads (or a mix of the two?)
- Do you want to see / do something specific? Visit historical places, ski, wine taste, hike, visit friends?
- What sort of weather do you hope to enjoy? (Warmer or colder).

- Do you want beach, forest or mountains? Or a mix?
- Are you travelling with family, and what do THEY want?

Once you've answered those questions, you can start narrowing your options. You will also have a rough idea of the radius of the area you can reach in your time frame (we'll get to the 90-day BREXIT restrictions shortly.)

I know many people get overwhelmed with booking a trip, so here's a run-through on how we chose our trip from the UK to Germany, using the questions above:

- We wanted to go away in April with our daughter (during the Easter school holidays).
- We had two weeks to travel (due to the school holidays).
- We were happy to pay to drive on motorways/ toll roads and then take smaller back roads to explore the area once we arrived.
- We wanted somewhere fun to ride our motorbikes.
- We wanted to see castles, history and waterfalls and we wanted to educate our teenage daughter on some European history.
- And we wanted to visit a foreign country.

With these parameters, most of Western Europe was open to us. We assessed our options and had a good look on Instagram and Pinterest for ideas of places to visit.

TOP TIP: This is a great idea if you're travelling with kids / teenagers: get them to research places they're excited to visit.

Eventually, the thoughts of Bratwurst and Black Forest Gateau won out and we decided to take our motorhome to Germany.

It could easily have been Holland, southern France, Austria, northern Germany, Belgium or Denmark; all of those fit within our parameters.
In the end, you have to just pick one and save the rest for another trip!

How to research a location

As soon as we decide on an area to visit, we start researching specific things to do/ see once we're there. **Type into Google** "Best things to do in_______ (in our case Southern Germany or the Black Forest.) Invariably 100 million results will be returned, but everything you need will normally be on the first page of Google.

Using something like a **TripAdvisor 'Best of' Board or a Tourist Information website** is perfect to get you started and see places to visit around your destination.

Start making a list of places which sound interesting; this will help you build up an itinerary later.

The other places to look for ideas are **Pinterest & Instagram.** Seriously, these are BRILLIANT for finding itineraries, ideas and cool places to see.

There are also lots of itineraries and country guides on the **Wandering Bird website** *(www.wandering-bird.com, under Destinations)* and you can join the Wandering Bird Facebook Group too, where people are constantly sharing great places they've visited.

WHY are you visiting?

The WHY of your visit can often help a lot with planning. We visited Germany to explore, but we also went to help our daughter out with her school homework. She needed to take photos of old buildings, castles and ruins and she was studying history in school. So that heavily influenced our potential destinations.
For you, it might simply be as easy as “I've never been there before” or “I like the wine, food or weather and I want to go back.” There doesn't need to be a serious and impressive reason to go anywhere.
After all, it (hopefully!) isn't going to be your last holiday- there'll be many more to enjoy.

WHEN are you visiting?

It may sound obvious, but the places you want to visit in the summer might not be the same in Spring or Winter.

And if you're forced to travel during the school holidays, it can also impact your decisions; some places are best avoided in busy periods (like the Italian Lakes!)

We want to travel up to Norway again to see the Northern Lights, which are only visible between October - March. So, it would be pointless putting that as our summer trip (although we have done Norway in summer and it's well worth the drive).

Similarly, if you want to go cycling or motorbiking on a specific mountain road, don't go in the winter when it's probably shut due to snow- we made that mistake with Stelvio Pass in Italy.

Consider the weather

In the UK, we're used to rain, cold and storms at random moments. But often, we seem to think Europe is warm ALL the time. Sadly, this is not true, and I know many people who have been caught out by freak snowstorms or heavy rain, especially in Spring or Autumn.

Make sure you check the weather a week or so before you travel and bring appropriate clothing. I always recommend taking something warm even if you're going on a holiday in the sunshine. Otherwise, you could find yourself heading up a mountain without appropriate clothing, which is what happened to us when we stopped at Mont Blanc on the way through to Italy. It was FREEZING, despite being in July.

And don't forget, if the forecast is awful, you can always change your plan and head elsewhere; that's the beauty of motorhome travel!

We've changed many itineraries based on actual and forecasted weather. In Scotland, we drove from the Isle of Skye up to the North-East coast to avoid the rain and had a magical day in the sun on Orkney.

Having said that, when we went to Norway for 3 weeks in July, it rained solidly almost every day. Sometimes you have to choose to go no matter what the weather is and make the best of it (how very British of me!)

What TYPE of trip do you want?

If you are travelling in the middle of August, it will be useful for you to decide as soon as possible how you want your motorhome holiday to go.

- Do you want to stay at a campsite which has loads of activities for the kids to do or which has a beach/ pool/ playground?
- Do you want to wild camp in your motorhome and stay at a new place each night, far from crowds and cities?
- Do you want to use aires / free overnight parking spots in Europe and stay 2/3 nights in a place before moving on?

To do that, it's helpful to understand a little more about the options for overnight stops, along with the pros and cons for each.

Where to Stay

In Europe, there are several options for overnight parking:

- Campsites
- Aires (also called Sostas/ Stellplatz)
- France Passion scheme or similar.
- Wild / free camping
- Staying on people's driveways (yep, for real).

Each has their pros & cons and we've used them all during our travels (except staying on someone's drive). **At this stage of planning,** you only need to decide if you're going to be travelling during school holidays and if you want to use a campsite or not.

If you DO, I highly recommend finding and booking one ASAP; the good campsites get booked up well in advance, especially near the beach.

Even outside the school holidays in the 'shoulder' months of June and September, campsites can be very busy indeed. Of course, if you do book a campsite in advance, changing your plans due to bad weather isn't so easy- it's a compromise.

Campsites

Campsites in Europe are exactly what you might expect: large motorhome/ camper parking areas, usually grassed with marked bays, facilities and a reception.

Some have more facilities than others. You can find campsites with their own beaches, or with private pools, restaurants, corner shops, entertainment, kids clubs, bike hire and surfboard lessons... the list goes on and on.

In the school holidays, if you're at a campsite and you don't have small children, you may find yourself **wondering what the heck you're doing with your life.**

Campsites in summer are generally loud, (despite any noise restrictions they say are in place.) Our worst nights in the motorhome EVER have all been spent in campsites, (both in the UK and Europe) and were awful thanks to thoughtless and overly noisy neighbours. There's a reason we prefer wild camping or using aires.

However, love them or hate them, campsites are incredibly useful. We use them fairly often as a safe place to leave the motorhome if we want to go exploring on our bikes. We'd rather pay £25 for a night (and use their facilities), than risk damage or worse to our van while we leave it unattended.

We have been known to check into a campsite, leave the van there for the afternoon while we explore on the motorbikes, then go back to the van and leave the campsite so we can wild camp somewhere for the night (we're weird like that!)

Europe doesn't seem to have as many 'adult only' campsites as the UK, although there are a few around-you just need to find them. And don't worry, despite the reputation some Europeans have, 'adult only' doesn't mean 'nudist' (just in case you were wondering!)

Some tips for using European campsites:

- Book EARLY, especially if there's a specific site you want to visit in the school holidays or if it's near a popular destination, like EuroDisney or a surfing beach.
- Try and park as far away from the pool/ restaurant / café / kids club / toilet block as you can if you want some quiet.
- Having said that, any large open space is going to become a football field, so that's not a great spot either unless you have kids.
- If we've made a reservation, we try to arrive later than usual at the site, so we can pick a place away from large groups or other dogs. The downside to this is not being able to choose if there's only one spot left- it's a delicate gamble.
- Not every campsite will allow you to choose a spot, but most do.
- Thefts occur on campsites. If you're going to leave towels/ swimsuits/ shoes etc outside to dry overnight, they may not be there in the morning. Some people have even had outdoor chairs and line-dryers stolen.
- Similarly, don't leave your van unlocked if you pop to the showers or go for a swim.

We prefer campsites on fields, where there is more room to relax, spread out and not all be on top of each other. However, there are very few of these in Europe- most campsites have clear pitch markings and not a lot of room during high season.

If you're travelling outside of the peak seasons, an ACSI Camping Card is a brilliant investment- you get discounts on many campsites and can save as much as 40% on some sites.

All campsites will want to see your passports / ID on arrival. Don't be alarmed if they retain them during your stay; this has happened several times to us and is normally for sites where you pay as you leave. Just remember to collect it before you go!

The simple fact is that if you want to stay in one place for longer than 48 hours, or you want continuous hook-up and/or facilities, you need to book a campsite.

Aires

Aires are magical places for anyone who wants to explore Europe in a motorhome or campervan. And they are unlike anything we have in the UK for motorhomes (although a few are springing up here and there).

Europeans like motorhomes. Heck, Europeans LOVE motorhomes. They make room for them, they encourage them and... wait for it... towns and villages **often**

provide dedicated parking areas for them that ARE NEAR PLACES you actually WANT to visit.

I'm serious. No more being stuck miles away from the nearest town and made to feel utterly unwanted wherever you go. *(I love the UK, but seriously, we could do so much better in this regard.)*

Europe wants you to bring your motorhome there. Europe encourages motorhome parking and motorhome travel and motorhome EVERYTHING. And it doesn't cost more than a few pounds a night at most. These places, provided and maintained by the local council, are called Aires in France and many other countries, Stellplatz in Germany, and Sostas in Italy.

One thing to understand is that 'aire' just means area in French. Literally. There are many types of aire in France and not all are suitable for motorhome parking, such as an aire de jeux (which is a children's play area).

Also, the motorway rest stop areas are also called aires (aires de repos). Now, motorway aires are BRILLIANT for getting fresh water and emptying waste (more on that later), but we don't recommend sleeping overnight here, even in the designated motorhome parking areas.

There are many stories of vandalism and theft to motorhomes camped overnight at motorway services, even while people are sleeping inside.

So, when we say 'aire', we mean places provided for motorhome parking near towns and villages, sometimes called 'aire de camping car'. These are normally well signposted using a picture of a motorhome, more on how to find them below.

Some tips for using Aires:

Aires are first-come, first-served, like a car park. You CANNOT book in advance (except for a few in the mountains during winter).

However, there are so many of them around that we've rarely had a problem finding a space. Try to arrive early in the afternoon if there's a specific one you want; most people tend to leave late morning and are situated by 3-4pm ready for the night.
They cost anywhere from nothing to around 15€/night (some services may be extra). Signs on the payment meter or notice board are usually very clear and easy to understand.
Normally, you buy a ticket from a machine (just like in a car park) and display it in your windscreen. Sometimes you pay at the shop, restaurant or business nearby.

Aires often have services like fresh water and waste disposal for an additional fee.
There normally isn't a barrier or a reception and you often won't find an electric supply, although some do for a fee.

NOTE: Caravans are NOT allowed to use Aires. If you are travelling with a caravan, a campsite is your only option unless you are happy to wild camp.

How to find Aires

We find aires in Europe using a couple of apps on our phone/ iPad:

- Park4night - worth paying for (also is a website).
- Campercontact- we use the free version.

There is a UK-based app called **Searchforsites** which is fantastic in the UK, but more limited for Europe.
You can also find aires using books which are updated and re-released every 12-24 months.
We prefer the apps to the books as changes are reflected more quickly; for example, if an aire is closed down for resurfacing or something, you might not know from a book.

Having said that, you will need internet to use the apps (more on internet later). If you don't have / want to use internet, a physical book is very useful.
You can find the best books & kit we recommend by scanning this QR code >>>

Other Overnight Schemes

Another parking scheme in France is France Passion, which is similar to the UK Brit Stops. This scheme offers FREE (once you've bought the yearly guide) overnight places to stop, usually on a business car park or land.

Places offered in the scheme include vineyards, restaurants, farms and even a snail farm! Businesses offer their land/ parking area for motorhomes/ vans to stay overnight, in exchange for you having a meal in their restaurant or taking a vineyard tour and buying some wine (or snails!).

Don't expect services – it's normally just a parking space in a car park or on someone's field. You probably won't find water or anywhere to empty waste.
It's not SUPPOSED to be a 'tit for tat' arrangement, but personally we felt uncomfortable the times we just wanted a drink in the restaurant and not a 3-course meal. We're also not big drinkers and don't visit a lot of vineyards, so it limited our options somewhat.

HOWEVER, if you love vineyards / farms / snails, these places are perfect for you; free overnight parking and the chance to do something you enjoy. It also means you don't need to worry about driving after a vineyard tour *"hic"*. Maybe buy a France Passion book and see if you use it enough to buy another one.

There are schemes like France Passion throughout Europe. I've included more details on them below:

- FRANCE - France Passion.
- GERMANY - Landvergnügen & WinzerAtlas.
- ITALY- incamperongusto.it & Agricamper.
- SWITZERLAND - Swiss Terroir.
- SPAIN - España Discovery.
- PORTUGAL - Portugal easy camp.
- SWEDEN - Swedestops.se
- DENMARK - Pintrip pintrip.eu
- NORWAY- Don't think they have (or need!) one. Wild camping is allowed almost everywhere- it's magical.

For everywhere else, or if you don't want to stay at someone's business, use Park4night or one of the other apps to find places to stay overnight.

As I mentioned earlier, there are some new schemes where people are offering out their driveway or field as a parking spot. We've never used these, so can't comment on what they're like.
I can potentially see the benefits in a town or city if you need to be somewhere specific, but out in the countryside I prefer to be away from people wherever possible and wouldn't like to be on someone's drive.

Wild / Free Camping

Ah, finally. Our favourite option… most of the time. There is some 'discussion' in the van life community that it should be called 'free or wild parking' or 'off-grid' camping. Call it whatever makes you happy. I often call it all three.

It's hard to explain what I love so much about wild camping; the freedom and feeling of no-one else in the world knowing where you are. The night sky. The quiet. Being self-sufficient (with a bed and a fridge and wifi!).

Yet, I was not always like this. When we started motorhoming, I'd never heard of wild camping- except in terms of crazy dudes with tents and big bushy beards. Or Bear Grylls.

When we got our first van and decided to head to Scotland to stay 'off-grid' for a few days, we had no idea how to find places, or manage our power in the van, or deal with finding water / waste disposal points. Heck, I didn't even know the terms to type into Google to try to figure it out.

The whole thing felt totally overwhelming and the thought of setting off on a journey and NOT knowing where we were spending the night gave me cold sweats. I hated the idea of driving around, lost, tired and forlorn, looking for somewhere safe to stay.

Over the years, we've built our confidence and experience until we're totally comfortable being off-grid

for several days at a time, with no plans for the following day.
Wild camping is tolerated in most countries in Europe with a motorhome or campervan, providing you follow these rules:

- Stay well away from areas where wild camping is prohibited (like the coastline in France).
- Stay away from private land and buildings, unless you have the owner's permission.
- Arrive late in the day (late afternoon at the very earliest) and leave by mid-morning.
- In most places, do NOT light a fire or BBQ. At all.

Our favourite way to find spots is again to use the Park4night website or app. (The same one as for the aires.)

Etiquette for Wild camping in Europe for motorhomes and campervans

So, how DO you actually wild camp? Here are some guidelines to help you:

- Don't put out tables / chairs / awnings. This is not a campsite (NOTE: we have used our outdoor chairs and BBQ a few times when we've been wild camping in the middle of nowhere. Use your judgement.)
- Don't make loud noise/ play loud music or be a nuisance.
- Clear up ALL litter and waste.

- Watch children and pets and don't let them wander away, wild camping doesn't mean there is no-one else around.
- Be sensible about safety. Lock doors and windows before going to sleep (there's a whole section on security later in this guide).
- If you're asked to move on, move on. This rarely happens if you're discreet but it is the price you pay for choosing not to use an aire or campsite. Remember, wild camping is NOT a right in most countries.

If wild camping is something you'd like to try but feel a bit intimidated by, we've created an in-depth guide for you, including:

- Step-by-step on how we find places.
- Why we choose to stay at some places and not others.
- How to set up your motorhome or van to stay off-grid.
- Staying safe.
- Places we've used around the UK & Europe and includes lots of tips for staying safe overnight.

Find out more at **wandering-bird.com/wild**

Wild camping in Germany

TAKE STOCK 1

I've thrown a lot of information at you already.
I don't want this guide to be overwhelming, so every now and then I'm going to have a break point like this to sum up what we've covered.

So far, we've talked about how to:

- Choose a destination that works for YOU.
- Decide on the structure of your trip.
- Choose the type of holiday you want.
- Looked at the various options for holidays/ overnight stops.

Of course, if you haven't got a set date for your trip, that's the first thing to figure out, and everything goes from there.

Practicalities

In the next section, we'll look at the practicalities of your trip, getting to Europe, planning a route and the essential kit you need to carry with you.

Getting to Europe

Once you've figured out where to go, you need to figure out HOW to get there.

If you're based in the UK, you have two ways of reaching mainland Europe with a vehicle: ferry or Eurotunnel.

There are pros and cons to each and we use both in different situations. No one way is better than the other; a lot depends upon your location in the UK, where you want to get to in Europe (hence us talking about that first!) and whether you're travelling with pets or not.

EUROTUNNEL

We love the Eurotunnel, but we actually use it less than the ferry. Let's list the pros and cons and then I can explain why.

Pros of the tunnel:

- Cheaper than most ferry routes (although not for the shorter ones).
- More flexibility on travel times.
- Quicker to cross.
- Better for pets.

- Can use Tesco Clubcard vouchers to pay!

Cons:

- Means driving all the way to Folkestone / Calais.
- No break from driving.
- Can't take any vehicles which use LPG as propulsion (having LPG for heating/ cooking is absolutely fine).
- Often LONG delays during school holidays.

FERRY:

There are several ferry routes which go from the UK to Europe. Most are run by either Brittany Ferries or DFDS. As with the Eurotunnel, there are pros and cons.

Pros of ferry:

- You get a rest while on the ferry, great if you have a long drive once you arrive in Europe. We especially like the overnight sailings.
- You can travel with a vehicle which uses LPG as a propulsion source.
- Usually there are fewer delays in summer.
- There are now pet-friendly cabins on some routes so you can take your dog inside with you.
- More convenient locations around the UK, which reduces driving distance; great for short trips.

Cons:

- Often more expensive.
- Usually only 2/3 sailings a day.
- Weather; storms on a ferry are not fun!

- Be careful of the Wi-Fi and the onboard phone network- it's EXPENSIVE. We put our phones on airplane mode to avoid accidental high connection charges.

Which do we prefer?

We travel regularly between the UK & Europe. Lately, we've been travelling a lot from the south coast of England to the west coast of France.
We tend to use Portsmouth to Caen ferry route as we like to use the pet-friendly cabins (we hate leaving our dog in the van), but these are often cancelled during winter. Still, it's usually more convenient for us to travel Portsmouth-Caen and back instead of driving to Dover and then all the way across to the west coast of France.

Strangely, both routes take about the same time, but we're much more rested when we use the ferry; driving all the way from Bordeaux to Portsmouth is exhausting! Having said that, if we're heading east in Europe, for example to Germany we almost always choose the tunnel; it's much more convenient for us, not to mention cheaper!

Whichever option you choose, book it up as soon as possible; it gets more expensive the closer to your travel date you get. Peak dates (such as the first day of holidays or last Sunday before school starts again) sell out VERY quickly.

Tre Cime di Lavaredo, Italian Dolomites

Essential Kit You Need

One of the things which caught us out when travelling to Europe for the first time was the essential kit you MUST carry in any vehicle (we don't have these rules in the UK.)

Obviously, there are some things you **should** carry in the UK, but in Europe they can (and do!) fine you if you don't have the legal gear.

NOTE: I'm going to assume your van is already equipped with the basics you need for travel;bedding, cutlery, clothes etc. If you're starting from scratch, **head to wandering-bird.com/gear for printable checklists (**there's also a list in the Appendices).

Here, I'm just talking about what you NEED to travel with a vehicle in Europe (this is mostly the same for motorhome, campervan or caravan & car.)

Essential Safety Equipment

- **Hi-vis reflective jackets – one per person** (These MUST be accessible without getting out of the vehicle; ie- don't keep them in the garage unless you can reach them from inside!)
- **Warning triangle** (one only is fine).
- **Headlight beam converters** – must be fitted to UK vehicles before driving in Europe.
- **UK vehicle sticker** attached to the back of vehicle or rear reg plates.
- **First aid kit** – compulsory in many European countries.
- **Red/ white warning board sign** – for anything overhanging the end of the motorhome or campervan (like a bike rack or storage box). These are not currently compulsory in France but ARE compulsory in Spain and Italy. Get the aluminium one for legality in Italy.

Do I need a breathalyser to drive in France or Europe?

Nope. This was a law France passed a few years ago and then quietly removed for whatever reason (or at least gave it a €0 penalty fee). Many posts ranking highly in Google still list a breathalyser in their kit list for France, but I promise you that you don't need one unless you want one. If you DO carry one, it must be in date.

Blind Spot Stickers

If your vehicle can legally weigh over 3.5tonnes and you're going to be travelling in or transiting built-up areas in France, you will need to display Angles Mort stickers. The stickers must use the official French-government design and there are strict rules about the size and position.

Other recommended kit to carry:

- Spare bulbs for all lights in the motorhome, internal & external.
- Torch
- Fire extinguisher / fire blanket.

Make sure you have the safety equipment required by each country you will be DRIVING THROUGH, not just the final one you are visiting.

If you need kit, find everything we recommend for European travel here >>>

Safety Kit you might need

The following kit are things you might legally need to carry in your motorhome or campervan, depending on when and where you are travelling.

- Snow chains/ winter tyres– check the rules on the country you are visiting and pay close attention to the DATES when the snow chain/ snow tyres rules come into force (see below for new France winter rules).
- Low Emission Zone stickers for many countries around Europe. You usually DO need to buy these several weeks in advance (see below.)
- Motorway toll tax/ Vignette. These are enforced in several countries across Europe, including Switzerland, Austria & Slovenia. You must have them fitted on your vehicle BEFORE you cross the border. You can buy them in garages near the border very easily, you don't need to buy these in advance.

Beware of Portugal, where you need to carry a temporary toll device in order to use the motorways. E-movis covers this (more on that later).

Tyres and snow chains

If you are planning to tour Europe in the winter, think about your tyres and snow chains. It's compulsory in most countries with mountains (France, Germany etc) to have winter tyres fitted and to carry snow chains which will fit onto your tyres. This is usually enforced between 01 November and 15 April but please do check in advance.

France winter tyre law

On 01 November 2021, a new law came into effect in France, stating a legal requirement to either have winter tyres fitted or to carry / wear snow chains where directed.

48 departments located in or near the French mountains (Alps, Corsica, Massif Central, Jura Mountains, Pyrenees, Massif Vosges) now have roads / regions where you **need to have winter tyres fitted or carry snow chains / socks** before driving on one of the regulated roads, regardless of weather conditions.

Nearly all the regions are in the south of France, but there is a map on Wandering Bird if you'd like to see them.

New signs will tell you when you're about to enter a compulsory equipment area. It's only compulsory between 01 November and 31 March each year; you can ignore the signs at other times (although there are B26 signs around which still insist on your having snow chains on high mountain roads with snow on them, even outside these dates.)

To comply, you must have one (at least) of the below:

- A full set of winter tyres (marked by mountains).
- Snow chains or snow socks for two driving wheels.
- Studded tyres

Heavy vehicles with a trailer must have BOTH winter tyres AND snow chains.

This law counts even if you're just passing through on the way to warmer climates. If you are found to not comply, you could be fined 135€ and/ or your vehicle could be impounded.

Personally, we use all-season tyres and carry snow chains. However, if/ when we plan to spend time skiing, we will upgrade the tyres to proper winter tyres for that period.

Low Emission Zones in Europe

There are several different types of Low Emission zones in both the UK and Europe:

- Some are closed to all vehicles of a certain emission category (more on that shortly).
- Some can only be entered with a Crit'air or similar sticker and need to be registered in advance or pay a fee within a short period of entering (usually 24 hours).
- Others can only be entered at certain times of the day/ week.

A vignette for tolls / motorway tax (used in Switzerland or Austria) is NOT the same as a low emission zone sticker.

A crit'air IS a form of low emission sticker, but only valid in France. You need different ones for different countries and usually they take 4-6 weeks to arrive so you need to order them way before you set of on your road trip.

NOTE: It is only one sticker per COUNTRY, not per city, so you should only need one for France, one for Germany etc.

And, don't forget, if you don't plan to enter any zones, you don't need a sticker at all.

How to find Low Emission Zones in Europe

The best way we've found is the Urban Access Regulations website, which has a map of all the zones and their type.

You can use this to plot your route and plan your road trip. You'll also find the correct government websites on there for where to buy your stickers. Don't use any site other than the official government website; you'll pay much more money than you need to!

Allow at least 4-6 weeks for your sticker to be delivered before you leave and make sure you read the instructions on where to put them in your windscreen carefully; it's usually lower RIGHT side, which is the driver's side for UK built vans. Don't block your view.

You will need access to your vehicle logbook in order to get a sticker. If you can't, or if you're hiring a vehicle without one, it is perfectly possible to avoid the zones- we've never ever had one!

Other Kit we recommend

We've been touring Europe for several years. We've tried all sorts of kit; some useful, some not so much.

Here is a list of things we highly recommend but are NOT essential.

I'll repeat, you do NOT legally need to carry any of these things. And if you are planning a lovely stay on a campsite with electric provided, I wouldn't worry about anything (except maybe the sat-nav).

The rest is more useful for people who will either be travelling a lot around Europe and/or staying away from campsites.

- **Motorhome sat-nav** – get one you can enter your motorhome dimensions into. See our favourites at **wandering-bird.com/gear.**
- Refillable gas bottles – One of the best upgrades we've done to our motorhome- (more on gas later).
- WiFi – more on that soon too.
- Toll pass – covered in the toll section.
- ACSI card – brilliant for discounted campsite prices if travelling outside peak season.
- Motorhome security devices.
- Solar panel – great if you're planning to stay off-grid.
- If you want to stay off-grid a lot, you might also benefit from a power-bank, generator and/or invertor.
- Exclusive Wandering Bird van-life logbook to record your adventures- this is possibly the most important of all! Get one at **wandering-bird.com/gear.**

Paperwork You Need

Ok, there is literally no way to make paperwork exciting. Sorry about that. I'm just going to rattle it off and get it over with as quick as possible.

If you're taking your own vehicle overseas, you'll need to carry the following paperwork for your vehicle:

- Vehicle Logbook (V5C) – **original** (take a photocopy as well).
- Vehicle insurance – must clearly show you're insured to drive in the country you're visiting.
- MOT (in date!) for vehicle – just being able to prove the date is fine; it's more for insurance if you have an accident.
- Breakdown cover – ideally store the emergency number and your client ID in your phone in case you need it quickly.
- Accident claim form for Europe (get from your insurer).

Green cards

UK driving licence holders do **not** need a green card when you drive in the EU (including Ireland), Andorra, Bosnia and Herzegovina, Iceland, Liechtenstein, Norway, Serbia, and Switzerland.
You may need to carry a green card to drive in other countries, including Turkey & Ukraine. Full details can be found on the uk.gov website.
NOTE: If you are towing a caravan or trailer, some (not all) countries in the EU will require a green card. Please check with your insurer and mention ALL countries you plan to pass through.

Trailer / Towing

If you are towing vehicles, a caravan or a trailer into Europe, you need to bring the following paperwork:

- EU trailer certification.

- Insurance for each vehicle being towed.
- MOT for each vehicle.
- Logbook for each vehicle.
- Green card for each vehicle AND the trailer / caravan (if required).
- Breakdown cover for each vehicle.

You must register commercial trailers over 750kg and all trailers over 3,500kg before you can drive through some countries in Europe. More information can be found on the gov.uk website or ask your insurer.

Passport

British passports (and most others) MUST have at least 6 months left on them before you enter the European Union. You MUST check that the expiry date is **ONLY 10 years from the date of issue, not longer.**
This is really important – many passports over the last 10+ years have been issued with an extra 9 months on them, but this will no longer be accepted by the EU.

So, if your passport was issued on 01 September 2015, it will expire (in the EU's eyes) on 31 August 2025, regardless of the actual expiry date.
(Ireland is the exception for this- you can travel to Ireland for the length of your current passport.)

YOU DO NOT NEED A BLUE PASSPORT – keep using your red one until you need to renew it, even if it says EU on the cover. However, you won't be able to use the EU citizen entry lanes at border control.

Driving Licence

Must be in date and you need the pink card part only. You must be authorised for the type of vehicle you are driving (i.e.- over 3.5 tonnes or not). Everyone who is planning to drive will need their own driving licence.

Health Insurance

One of the big changes of BREXIT is the reciprocal health agreements for treatment abroad. The EHIC is still valid (if you have one in date) but you may find you need additional travel/ health insurance.
It's also worth carrying details of any vaccinations or injections you've had or medication you use – just in case. If you have to carry a lot of medication, you might need a letter from your doctor- please ask them for guidance.

Travel Insurance

Make sure you have an insurance policy in place which covers your personal items, such as jewellery, phones or laptops. Many house insurance policies cover this, but if not grab a policy before you leave. You also want to ensure you can get home again should anything happen; how will you, your family AND your vehicle get back if you are unable to drive?

Visa (if you need one)

In 2022, UK citizens do not need a visa to visit Europe, but this will apparently change in the near future. Many other countries do need one, so check in advance. (We'll discuss the length of time you can stay shortly.)

Proof of return/onward travel & location of stay

Some countries require details of where you will be staying. If you've booked a campsite/ hotel in advance, have those details to hand. If you're planning to use aires/ wild camp, just say you will be using an aire near "_____" (don't say wild camping!)

Also, EU border officials could ask to see proof of onward / return travel – such as a date of ferry crossing back to the UK.
To date, we don't know of any motorhome travellers who have been asked for details of stay, return travel or funds, so please don't worry about it too much; they seem to accept motorhomers are self-sufficient.

PETS – Pet paperwork is discussed in the Pet Travel section.

Vignettes for motorway tax

Some countries in Europe don't have tolls, they ask you to buy a 'vignette' in order to pay to use the motorways / major roads.
In countries which use vignettes, you will need to buy a separate vignette for each vehicle **which will be on the road,** but not if they will be staying on the trailer (if you're just passing through).
HOWEVER, you will also need a vignette for the trailer. If in doubt, ask at the point of sale – they normally speak excellent English.

Red / White sign on cycle rack / tow

I mentioned this a little earlier but wanted to reiterate it. If you are visiting Spain or Italy and have anything extending past the back of your motorhome (including bicycles strapped to the back) you NEED to have a red/white striped sign.

We have a storage box on a bike rack and strap the sign to the box. Italy states needing an aluminium one but we've never had this checked.
Make sure the lines of your board are **pointing into the middle of the road.**

Hiring a Vehicle

If you are hiring a motorhome or camper in Europe, it is YOUR responsibility to make sure the vehicle has the required safety equipment. The on-the-spot fines apply to you as the driver, not the company.

Check in advance with the company what kit they will provide with the vehicle and what you will need to bring/ buy when you arrive. You may need to bring a DVLA code and / or an International Driving Permit.

Take a list of what is legally required with you and check it off one by one as you are given the handover. Do not drive until you are happy you comply with the local laws.

Make sure you have proof that you can take the vehicle across a border into another country if that's what you're planning to do. Normally this is a letter which has several translations of the local languages on it.

For more help with hiring a vehicle, what to check before booking and where to get good deals, head to **wandering-bird.com/gear or use this QR code >>>**

Pet Travel

We travel back and forth to Europe almost monthly with our cocker spaniel, Mac. Sadly, since BREXIT, this is one area which has become considerably worse and there have been many changes.

FIRSTLY... your UK Pet passport is no longer valid. Sorry.

To get from UK to Europe. your pet needs (on top of the 'normal' injections given to dogs when they're young):

- An Animal Health Certificate – must be issued before EVERY trip.
- Rabies vaccination.
- Microchip

Animal Health Certificates

These are now issued in place of a Pet Passport. They can be issued up to 10 days before you travel and are valid for up to 4 months, but only for one trip- i.e., every time you return to the UK and then want to leave again, you'll need another one.

To get one, you will need to make an appointment with an authorised vet (not all are) and bring:

- Your dog.
- Your pet's microchip details.
- Your pet's vaccination history and rabies jab date.

Rabies Jab

One bit of good news is that you no longer need a blood test to prove that the rabies jab has been effective – all that is needed is a rabies injection at least 21 full days before travel.

Tapeworm

If you are travelling with your dog from the UK directly to Finland, Republic of Ireland, NI, Norway or Malta, they must have treatment against tapeworm (Echinococcus multilocularis) between 1-5 days before arriving in country.

IRELAND – Ireland is working to make this process easier for UK residents. The **DAERA website** has all the up-to-date details so check this before travel. In 2022, it is necessary to get a tapeworm administered by a vet before you visit Ireland.

Returning from Europe back to the UK

The process of returning from Europe to the UK hasn't changed.
Your dog will need a worming tablet **administered by an approved vet** 1-5 days before your return to the UK. They will sign and stamp the animal health certificate to show it's been done. NO, sadly you cannot do it yourself.

When we first had to do this, it was intimidating, especially having to phone and visit a vet in a foreign country. However, we've been doing it for years and it's honestly very easy. We try to find somewhere about 4 days before we're due to go back to the UK, which gives us a little wiggle room.

Most vets near the British border are used to 'walk-ins' and will do their best to fit you in, (although not every vet can accept walk-ins, so phoning in advance is best if you're not staying in the area.)

Europe Travel - Legalities

How long can you stay in Europe?

Ok, here comes the fun part. *NOTE: This is for UK passport holders who are resident in the UK. For anyone else, please check your embassy online.*

UK residents can now stay in the Schengen area for 90 days in every **rolling period of 180 days**. You can either use that time all at once (then you need to leave the area for a clear 90 days) or you can take several smaller trips, keeping an eye on your dates so you don't stay too long in total. Your passport will be stamped on entry and overstaying your welcome could see you banned from entering the Schengen area again in the future!

The Schengen area includes the whole of the EU PLUS Iceland, Liechtenstein, Norway and Switzerland.
NOTE: Croatia joined the Schengen Area in January 2023.
These countries are not included and therefore you can visit each for 90 days each on top of your 90 days in the Schengen area:

- Bulgaria
- Cyprus
- Romania
- Morocco
- Ireland (currently allows unlimited visits for UK nationals)

ALCOHOL / CIGARETTES

There are restrictions on how many duty-free products you can bring with you from Europe into the UK.
The latest guidelines can be found on the GOV.UK website

TAKING MEAT / MILK OUT OF UK

Similarly, there are restrictions on what animal products you can take OUT of the UK, including products containing meat and milk.
There is some allowance for baby products and special-issue pet foods, but otherwise you need to be very careful what you pack and carry with you across the border.

Our experience

I think most people heard the news story of the lorry drivers who had their ham sandwiches confiscated when the BREXIT rules first came into effect.

Since then, we've crossed the border both ways several times and have at times accidentally carried dry & tinned dog food, several cans of chilli and other meat products and some Dairy Milk chocolate (and Jaffa Cakes!)
We've never hidden them and we accept that we might get them confiscated if officials feel the need. However, not once has this happened. Do with that information what you will…

Route Planning

Ok, so now you know where you're going, how to get to Europe and what you need, the next task is to figure out your plan and route.
There are several ways of doing this and there is no 'right way'. I'll share what we do in the hopes it might help you, but if not, do what feels right for you.

Bear in mind that we drive every 2/3 days and prefer to use aires / wild camp, so we don't have to worry about campsites very often. Obviously, if you're booking campsites, you'll need to plan in a bit more detail so you can book them up.

One thing to note is that we rarely plan an actual road route until we're driving or setting off for the day. **I don't plan the roads in advance** – just the places we want to visit during our trip. Everything else I do as we travel. If we want to visit a specific aire or campsite, I'll note that in our plan.

Using the Maps App

When we are planning a trip, one of the first things I do is open the 'Maps' app on my iPhone. (NOTE: this is NOT the same as Google Maps.)

Using 'Maps' I can then start a new collection for our trip and save all the places we've found that we want to visit. Then, I can see where they are in relation to each other. These are the places I found on Pinterest, Instagram or Google. From here, I find it easy to see a rough route we should follow in order to see everything we want to.

Of course, you can also do this on a physical map if you find it easier – whatever works for you. Either way, the point is to create a list of places to visit or stay and then decide the order in which you want to visit them.
Make sure to allow time for 'no-driving' days and don't plan to drive too far. We used to try to cram far too much in and end up returning from a trip needing a new holiday!

At least every 3/4 days we have a rest day. Mr WB does most of the driving (his choice) and although he says driving the motorhome is 'more comfortable than the car', he still appreciates a no-driving day.
We also make time for exploring and relaxing days. Don't underestimate how tiring road trips can be, especially if you're moving around regularly.
Be sure to take into account the roads you'll be driving on. 60 miles around the coast in Norway will take you two hours (maybe longer), while on an autobahn in Germany

it could take less than an hour. If in doubt, err on the side of caution and plan less driving.

Tolls in Europe

Many people are concerned about tolls in Europe and like to plan their routes to avoid them. There are pros and cons to this. Tolls occur in nearly every European country which doesn't insist on a vignette. Germany has some free autobahns and some paid, as does Holland.

When you plan a route in a country without a vignette, you have two options:

- The quick way (which uses tolls roads when necessary).
- The cheap way (which doesn't!)

There is no right answer – it's whatever's best for you. If you only have a week for your holiday, many people will want to get to their destination ASAP, which means using toll roads.

If you have more time, you may want to save money and take the slower (but usually prettier) back roads.
If you want to get an idea on how much a toll route might cost, use the website viamichelin.com/

This great site will tell you the approximate driving costs for your trip, both in fuel consumption and tolls. The fuel setting is annoying as you can't select for a motorhome/

camper, although you can select the appropriate mpg, but the toll charges & vignette costs (as long as you are under 3.5 tonnes and under 3m tall) are very accurate.

The same site will also show you the best (and cheapest) routes. For example, route 1 from Calais to Zagreb will cost 20.95€ in tolls, plus a 24.20€ vignette (tax disk), while route 2 is roughly the same distance, but will cost 60.84€ tolls PLUS the 24.20€ vignette for Austria.

Tips to make the tolls in Europe cheaper & easier

Ideally, you want your motorhome to be under 3m tall – any higher puts you as a Cat 4 commercial vehicle and toll charges are much higher. This is one of the biggest reasons we downsized our motorhome to a lower profile one.

On some tolls, any vehicle with 3 axles (ie, towing a trailer or very long), will be a Class 3, but as most tolls are automatic, they don't register it.
Most tolls accept cards, but some have issues with UK-issued cards, so carry cash and coins in local currency (remember, not everywhere in Europe uses Euros). Also, queues for 'cash only' lanes are often less than card lanes, which can help when it's busy.

Does left/ right-handed drive matter?

Usually, it doesn't matter a jot whether you're in a left or right-handed motorhome or van in Europe, especially if there are two of you.

However, if you're on your own, the tolls can be a bit of a pain if you're in a UK vehicle (i.e. steering wheel on the right side of the vehicle) as the toll booth will be on the opposite side (same for car parks).

We combat this by using a toll pass; however, there are plenty of people who park up and nip outside their vehicle to go pay the toll, so don't be embarrassed about it.

Get a Toll Pass

We love having a toll pass- it makes life so much easier. We use e-Movis in much of Europe, which allows us to go through the toll 'quick' lanes without stopping to pay and send us a bill at the end of the month for whatever tolls we've used.

This has saved us SO much time, especially in summer when queues at toll stops can be huge. It's not an essential motorhome accessory, and you can happily tour Europe without it, but it really does help speed things up.
Apparently, e-Movis allow vehicles up to 7.5t to use their toll passes- contact them for further advice.

Things to check before you go

On our very first trip to Europe with our motorhome, we nearly died. I'm not even kidding.
We had been travelling around Italy and detoured up into the Alps to explore Switzerland (and get away from the crowds). On our second or third mountain pass, our brakes failed. Like, failed failed.

Suddenly, we were hurtling down a mountain, at increasing speed, with multiple hairpin bends... and an unbraked trailer behind us with 2 heavy motorbikes on it. We had no way of slowing down apart from the handbrake.
I'm not even going to try and sugar coat it – it was hands down one of the scariest moments of my life. I am forever grateful that Mr WB was driving and that he understands engine braking, and that our handbrake was enough to slow us down.

By pure fluke, there was a town at the bottom of the mountain with a garage. We pulled into the car park in a cloud of steam & smoke and terrified faces. I don't think I'd said a word for 20 minutes. The garage owner, (who didn't speak a word of English; why should he?), came out, wiped his hands, looked at us and said 'oh'. Oh indeed.
It turns out that our newly bought motorhome (we'd only owned it for 3 months) hadn't been serviced properly as

we'd been told, and the brake fluid had been topped up with water.
This water then got hot as we used the brakes on the mountains and evaporated, leaving us with no brake fluid... and therefore no brakes!

Now, in all honesty, there's not a lot we could have done about this. We were told the vehicle had been serviced and we had no reason to doubt the dealer.
But now we get our van checked before every big trip and we vary the garages we use as well... just in case!

Things to check on your motorhome before you go include:

- Oil (and maybe carry some spare with you).
- Brakes & Brake fluid.
- Tyres
- Windscreen wash
- Batteries
- Locks (doors and windows).
- Lights for vehicle inside & out (carry spares).
- Trailer lights (carry spare bulbs).
- Gas bottles (more on that very soon!)
- Ideally pop to a campsite for a night to test the electric hook up (EHU), fridge, heating & cooker - all the things which may have developed gremlins if you don't use your motorhome regularly.
-

You CAN get things fixed in Europe if you need to, but it's a lot easier to get them fixed before you go.

Our second Motorhome in Austria

TAKE STOCK 2

Ok, we've reached the end of everything you need to know/ do before you go.
I hope the information above has answered many of your questions, but don't worry if you're feeling overwhelmed; I've just given you 4+ years' worth of knowledge in 60 pages!

Remember – you're not SUPPOSED to know all this stuff by heart yet- that's the beauty of a guide like this; you can keep it with you and refer back to it as often as you need to.

This section, we covered:

- How to get to Europe.
- Essential kit you need to carry.
- Paperwork to bring.
- Pet travel.
- Planning a route & tolls.
- Things to check before you leave.

Now comes the fun part- life on the road in Europe! I'll be sharing lots of tips for how to make your trip easier and find what you need.

Life on the Road

Europe Travel Tips

This seems as good a place as any to share some general Europe travel tips for anyone who has not been before.

Headsets

Firstly, it is illegal in many European countries to use a headset whilst driving, even with a hands-free kit. It needs to be on speakerphone in your car. I don't know how strictly this is enforced, but it's worth knowing.

Breakdown

Breakdown cover is essential in Europe. Make sure your breakdown covers towing to somewhere which could help fix the problem and covers the cost of a hotel for you if you need to vacate your van for a few days.

Also, some well-known breakdown companies have recently changed their policies so that they no longer cover vehicles over 3.5 tonnes. Please check your policy carefully and call them to check if you're in doubt.

Bank charges

This is something we didn't think about until after our first European road trip- which meant that we paid a fee on every single bank transaction – doh!

We have now switched to an account which doesn't charge for foreign payments and if you travel regularly, it might be worth looking at.

Your bank might need to know that you're going abroad, especially if you don't go regularly. Otherwise, you run the risk of them blocking your transactions.

Many banks accept notice to travel over online banking – you might be able to do this via an app or by logging in to your online account.

On the subject of banks, UK cards are generally accepted everywhere in Europe, although American Express not so much. However, some countries, most notably the Netherlands, only accept Maestro. It's unclear why, but it's very frustrating. If you don't have Maestro, you'll need to carry cash.

Emergency numbers

112 is the emergency number for all over Europe. There are national emergency numbers in each country (like 999 in UK) but dial 112 and you'll get through to whatever service you need. I believe there is an English speaker at every unit, so you should get through to someone who can help.

The mobile will pick up the strongest signal irrespective of your supplier. More importantly, the signal can be triangulated. The operator will know exactly where you are in an emergency.

And yes, you can dial it from any UK mobile, as long as it is connected to a network. I believe it may sometimes work even without a network.

Medication

If you are carrying a large amount of medication with you, make sure you have a doctor's note clearly stating what the medication is and what it's for. This can be in English but should be stamped & dated.

Time Zone

Much of Western Europe (including France) is one hour ahead of the UK. Their clocks go forward and back at the same time as the UK, so they always stay one hour ahead. Of course, the further East you travel, the further ahead the time zone gets. Don't be caught out by Portugal, which is the same as the UK.

It can be confusing to know what time zone you're in when you cross a border. If you're catching a ferry or have an appointment, check VERY carefully. (A quick Google search for "Time in ___" is all you need.)

Alternatively, in the Clock function of most smartphones you can set 'Zones / World Clock'. You can see UK time and the country you are in. Helps know what time it is back home.

Tipping

If you decide to treat yourself to a meal out, most restaurants will include a tip in the bill. Otherwise, 10-15% is usually standard. Coffee shops and lunchtime eateries often don't include a tip, so check your bill before paying.

Stop signs

Stop means STOP. You must come to a complete stop at a stop sign before setting off. Some recommendations are to wait for 3 seconds, in case any police are watching.

Beware of parked cars on the sides of fast roads

Entrapment is allowed in much of Europe and police will regularly park an old car at the side of the road with a hidden camera in it, and then pull you over further down and give you a speeding ticket, which must be paid there and then (more on this shortly)

Speed camera warnings

If you see a sign for a speed camera, there's nearly always a camera within a mile for sure; this is especially true in France.

Drones

If you have a drone, check the rules and requirements for each country you might fly in. Ideally, print them out so you can remember. Your drone will need your ID and you possibly need a licence to fly.

Driving in Europe

Don't be intimidated by driving in Europe... although I know that's easier said than done if you've never done it before.

Here are a few tips we've picked up along the way:

- You'll be driving on the right of the road.
- You DON'T need a left-hand drive vehicle although it might help if you're travelling on your own.
- The road system is set up for you driving on the right. Signs are on that side, roundabouts have helpful arrows and slip roads are pointed the right way. It's not as hard as it sounds.
- Avoid driving in Paris. At all times. In any vehicle. It's crazy.
- France still has the 'prioritie a droite' rule at a few random roundabouts, (which meant you had to stop ON the roundabout for anyone coming onto it...!) It is sign-posted where it exists, but most places have removed it. HOWEVER, expect the occasional older French resident to merrily sail onto the roundabout and expect you to stop for them. It's fun!

Getting Fuel

Many people worry whether they should fill up in the UK or Europe.

In our experience, Europe is often a little cheaper, BUT Europe (especially France) often has fuel strikes with very little notice, especially during the holidays. We ALWAYS fill up in the UK before we go... just in case.

Fines in Europe

In most places in Europe, it is perfectly legal for the Police to stop you on the side of the road and demand instant payment if you are caught speeding (or breaking any other rule).
They accept cash (or cheque in local currency), and if you do not have it they will drive you to the nearest cashpoint to extract the correct amount.

They also don't give change. I know someone who was fined 90€ for speeding, only had 5 x 20€ on them... and had to be escorted in the police vehicle to the cash machine to get 10€ change!
You can get fines for all sorts of things. Normally, it will be due to speeding, or not having a correct country sticker or a broken light. Then, when they stop you, they will ask to see all the paperwork and maybe things like your hi-vis jackets and logbook.

Also, in a motorhome you could be escorted to a weigh bridge, so please make sure you are under the legal maximum weight of the vehicle, which includes all passengers! If you are over the maximum allowed weight, you will need to remove items from the van until you are legal to drive off; you will have to leave those items behind forever.

Money Money Money

Most of Europe uses Euros. Everywhere. No other currency is accepted. (Some people seem to think they can pay with USD or GBP instead of Euro; you can't, although you can usually use a foreign bank card and accept the exchange rate charges.)

Always carry Euros with you. We carry around 100€ in cash, as well as keeping all our 2€, 1€ and 50c coins to use in the fresh water and waste units.

The countries in Europe which DON'T use Euros are:

- United Kingdom (which does NOT include southern Ireland- they use Euros).
- Bulgaria – Lev
- Czech Republic – Koruna
- Denmark – Krone
- Hungary – Forint
- Norway- Krone
- Poland – Zloty
- Romania – Leu
- Switzerland – Swiss Franc CHF

NOTE: As of January 2023, Croatia use the Euro

We have found it very difficult to get foreign money out in Europe as many places require you to order it a week in advance! Try and bring currency with you where possible. If you need some quickly, an airport is a good place to try.

Also, be warned that the Netherlands is a pain for accepting no other cards except Maestro. Even Visa debit cards are rejected in many places. So, either get a Maestro card or be prepared to carry a chunk of cash.

Getting LPG (gas) in Europe

Our BIG gas mistake...

Once upon a time, in March 2018, we headed to Europe in our motorhome. I had just quit my job so we could travel more, and we were feeling buoyant.

We were chilling out in France, making a cup of tea when the gas hob spluttered and died. “Not a problem,” we thought. “We have another bottle...”

However, upon checking we discovered that we had forgotten to replace our old bottle and the one we had was empty. So we had no gas at all and needed to buy a new gas bottle.

However, that's not as easy as it sounds in Europe because:

- You **can't exchange** UK gas bottles in Europe (nowhere will accept them).
- You **can't refill** exchangeable UK gas bottles in Europe (some places say they can do this, but it's often not legal, so be VERY careful.)
- You **CAN refill refillable** gas bottles if you have the appropriate connectors, but we didn’t HAVE any refillable bottles on our van.

Also, if you buy a French (or European) gas bottle, they don't fit the fittings of a UK system! You need a whole new system of connectors and pigtails.

Even better, if you have the system set up for French gas bottles and then pop over to Germany, the bottles there don't use the same connectors as the French OR UK ones, you need a totally different set of connectors.

In total, there are 3 (4 including the UK) types of gas connectors for Europe.

So, how do you get gas in Europe?

These are the options available to UK motorhomes, campervans and caravans:

1- Bring Enough Gas with you

Option 1 is straightforward if you're going on a week or even a two-week holiday: bring enough gas from the UK. We carry a 6kg and an 11kg bottle and **these EASILY last us 2 weeks during summer.**

However, they last us less than a week in winter. We use roughly 4 kg of gas in 24 hours in winter when it's really cold.

2- Refillable gas bottle system (LPG)

If you're going to be touring Europe a lot with your motorhome or camper, we highly recommend getting a refillable gas system fitted to your van.

Throughout Europe (and the UK), there are easy-to-use LPG (usually called GPL in Europe) refill stations in some petrol stations, especially on motorways.

To use these, you just pull in, get the hose with the nozzle on and refill your tanks.

Yes, some stations have recently closed in the UK, which is frustrating, but LPG will never disappear completely whilst there are cars around which use it for fuel; you just might need to travel a little further to find a station.
More info on using and finding refillable gas systems is below.

3- Install a fitted LPG tank
We considered this option, but for us it made more sense to get bottles as we plan to visit some countries where finding refillable gas is apparently very difficult, like Morocco.

In these places, we can take one of our refillable gas bottles out, strap it somewhere safe on the back of the van and connect an exchangeable bottle instead that we buy as needed.
We also didn't have a lot of space under our van as we had hydraulic legs fitted (we don't on our new van, but we're used to refillable bottles now.)

4- Use exchangeable gas bottles in each country
Of course, you can buy exchangeable gas bottles in each country you visit. This works in the same way as the UK- you buy a bottle, then swap it for another one (in the same country).

This is how we managed to fix our 'no gas' predicament: we were able to buy a bottle and a correct pigtail from a campervan shop- thank goodness! We had to spend one night without eating (in March) and it was COLD!

However, this is an expensive way to travel for long periods. You need to sign a contract & pay for a new bottle (plus pay a deposit) each time and you can't exchange the bottle unless you are staying in that one country (unusual for long trips), meaning you'll lose your deposit each time.

TOP TIP: some places will ask for an address in that country- you can use a local campsite.

Obviously, you'll need to carry the correct pigtails for each country as well so you can connect them to your UK system. We highly recommend buying these in advance as not every camping shop in Europe stocks them, especially not ones to fit onto a UK system.
Gas bottles are commonly sold in garages, especially big supermarkets. You will occasionally find them at the bigger service stations on motorways.

5- Don't use any gas
Option 5 – don't use any gas in your van. Stay on campsites and use electricity and electric cooking / kettle etc. This is fine if you're never planning to use aires or wild camp, but it means getting an electric hob / oven (most are gas) and also means you are forever

tied to electric. For us, that isn't a feasible option. What if the campsite trips out?

How much gas do you need for a road trip?

When we toured Italy for two weeks in August, we didn't need to change our gas bottles at all. We cooked with gas most nights, made countless brews (my husband is a hot drink addict), used lots of hot water for washing up and showers (there were 3 of us), ran our fridge on gas and we didn't even come close to using the 12kgs (2 x 6kg bottles) we had with us.

The thing which REALLY cripples our gas consumption is when we have the heating on. In winter, we can use a 6kg bottle in 2 days when it's really cold and the heating is running 24/7.

So, think about the length of your trip and the weather (will you need heating and does your heating run on gas?) If in doubt and if you plan to use your van a lot, I always recommend changing your system for a refillable one; it's so much easier to use and reduces the worry about running out.

NOTE: If you do fit refillable gas bottles, you should get them checked professionally and tell your insurance. This applies to any changes you make to systems on your van.

If you're hiring a vehicle, you'll need to check with them about what gas and connectors they supply, especially if you're planning to visit different countries.

Remember that Europe observes Sunday trading laws and many businesses (including camping shops) will be closed on a Sunday, so plan your shopping and gas buying in advance if not refillable.

If you can, run two bottles but we don't advocate using the auto switch over; yes, it's annoying at 3am when the heating cuts out and you think you're going to freeze in your bed... but at least you KNOW one bottle is now empty and therefore you need to exchange it or find an LPG station to fill up.
We've heard so many stories of people who didn't realise the bottles had switched over and found themselves in the middle of nowhere with no gas. *(We would never do that...!)*

Using Refillable gas bottles in Europe

We have now fitted the Gaslow LPG refillable bottle system on our last two motorhomes and it's brilliant. We've used it throughout Europe, including up in Norway and down to Croatia.

Finland
Finland currently doesn't seem to have LPG stations at ALL (neither does Morocco) so you need to make sure you fill up before you head that way and have an option to connect a new exchangeable bottle if needed.

How to find LPG stations in Europe

To find LPG stations in Europe, we use the website: https://www.mylpg.eu/stations/
In Norway, there is a website called: http://www.lpgnorge.no/stasjonsoversikt/english
The mylpg.eu Europe map does have some places which are out of date, so use with caution, but we've always found one eventually. Again, don't wait until you're desperate to fill up, we stop and refill when it's about half empty.

How to use an LPG filling station

You refill with LPG almost exactly like you do with fuel. Find a filling station (LPG is normally at a separate pump on its own out of the way but is sometimes hidden in the middle (in the most awkward spots for motorhomes!)

Pull in, open the filler, connect the hose and press the button. Sometimes you might need to ask the clerk on the desk to turn the pump on. Keep a close eye on the level when you are filling and don't overfill or rely on the auto cut-off.

CAUTION: there will be a sharp blast of gas when you disconnect. It makes me jump every time. Make sure your hands are covered- wearing gloves is a good idea.

Using the Channel Tunnel if your van has LPG tanks fitted

If your motorhome has LPG fitted for use as fuel, even if it can be switched off completely, you are NOT allowed on the Eurotunnel. Ferry only, I'm afraid.

If you have refillable LPG tanks fitted for use as domestic gas, then you CAN travel on the Channel Tunnel. Expect them to stop you and check that the tanks are turned off as you are boarding.

Yes, that means your fridge will need to be turned off for the duration of the trip, so don't stock up too much food before you travel unless you put some ice packs or frozen peas in there to keep it all cool. After all, it's only 60 minutes or so and you don't need to turn it off until you are waiting to board.

Just remember to turn it on again on the other side...

I've heard some European stations don't let you fill up with gas...

This is both true... and false.

European laws on using refillable gas are strict (as is the UK) and the types of tanks which are allowed to be refilled are strictly regulated.

If you don't have a filler on the outside of your motorhome (which we don't on our latest van), it can be hard for the cashier to see what you're filling, so they stop the flow and come check.

But they'll usually turn it on again once they're happy. We have heard occasional stories of someone being refused LPG because they have an internal filler; this seems to happen more in Spain, so fill up before you arrive then try the bigger stations.

Finding Water

Finding fresh drinking water for your motorhome / campervan is a LOT easier in Europe than it is in the UK. Promise.
There has only been one time in all our travelling where we've had trouble finding water.
That was in Norway, around Fläm, and we had to drive about half an hour out of our way to get water because the local refill point was broken and the nearby campsite refused to let us fill up even when we offered to pay. Grrr.

But most places in Europe have plenty of options. You can find them on the Park4night app. You can also fill up at campsites if you're using them or use the motorway services (aires de service); many of these have water and waste disposal. Many local village aires also have service points (again, we look on Park4night to find ones which do.)

It will cost around 2€ for a tank of fresh water and another 2€ for toilet waste disposal. You can normally dispose of your grey waste water over a grate for free. You'll need your own hose and connectors to get fresh water; don't forget to take them with you afterwards!

If you're going to be using campsites a lot, you might want to buy a LONG water hose. Many times, there are only a couple of taps for the site and the tap can be far away, so getting water becomes a 'faff'.
You can either roll away your awning, pack up your stuff, drive to the tap and fill up your van OR, carry a really long hose and use that. Just be aware you will be expected to stop filling for anyone who wants to fill a jug or water bottle.

The other option is a collapsible container. We have a 15l collapsible jug that we can fill and use to pour water into the tank without any problems. Sometimes, this is easier than the hose but takes longer.

Doing Laundry

It's one of the questions we get asked the most- How do you wash laundry while travelling?
Admittedly, some of us pack more clothes than others *looks innocent* so it's usually my husband who starts

the process, by casually commenting that he is down to his last set of underwear.

"Oh," I reply, whilst wondering why on earth he couldn't learn to give me at least a day's notice on this stuff. *Van-life - it requires more patience than you ever knew you had!!*

So then I need to find somewhere to wash clothes. Quickly.

There are several options available:

- Handwashing, normally in a sink or a bucket.
- Laundry tub or bag onboard.
- Laundrette at campsite.
- Coin-operated laundromat.
- Paid Laundry service.

As with everything, there are pros and cons to each.

If you're hand / bag / tub washing on your van, you'll need to find somewhere to dry your clothes.

In a motorhome, you can pack a portable line dryer; many fold down flat. Alternatively, just drape your clothes all over the inside and/ or outside of the van, especially if you have a bike rack.
However, be aware some 'posher' campsites don't allow laundry hanging outside, even swimwear. Usually, we dry our washing in our bathroom which luckily has a

heating vent, so we can turn the heating on and everything dries overnight- a feature we love, especially in winter.
Be cautious if you leave your clothes outside overnight- many people have had things stolen by passers-by.

Laundry services are an easy option if you can find a good one. However, there have been tales of travellers with excellent taste in underwear losing their fancy knickers & not having any proof that they were in there.

Also, laundry services can take a few days, so they only really work if you're staying somewhere for a while.

Our favourite option is the humble laundrette (either on a campsite or in a nearby town). It's been relatively easy to find one so far, and they're cheap (6-10€), quick (done within 90 minutes) and we can plan it around our travels… usually!

(Seriously, I think I need to start hiding a pair of his boxers and socks for emergency use! Actually, that's a great idea. Excuse me…)

Finding a Laundrette

I have discovered a fairly easy way to find a laundrette near to us anywhere in Europe- think like an American. Don't type into Google 'where can I wash my clothes?' or 'laundrette near me' (although that last one does sometimes work), but instead use phrases like 'coin-operated laundromat near me' or 'coin-operated

laundromat in _____' (insert name of largish town. If that doesn't work- choose a bigger town!)
You can also search 'laundromat' in Google Maps to see options near you.
Most large towns and cities have one, if not several, laundrettes. Local people use & rely on these to do their own washing all over the world.
Other places which often have laundry facilities are campsites and also many large supermarkets in Europe. (A trend which seems to be catching on in the UK.)
A company called Revolution seem to run most of them, if you Google them you'll find a map of places with outside laundry facilities so you can put a wash on while you shop.
TOP TIP: Most people use these after work, so you'll find them emptier during the day.
Also, many laundrettes don't take cards (same for ones on a campsite) so save your 1€ coins to use here, but you'll probably need your own detergent and softener.

Using Mobile Phones in Europe

Firstly, **make sure your UK mobile is unlocked** before you go to Europe. If you're not sure if it has already been done, pop into your local network store and get it done properly.

ROAMING

Getting rid of roaming charges for foreign phones when travelling was an EU initiative, not a UK one. Now that the UK has left the EU, UK networks are charging you again for using your phone abroad.

All the major networks now charge for making phone calls / texts and using data. The cost varies depending on your monthly plan, but the average is around £2/day.

Also, it's important to note that, just because you have unlimited data on your phone / iPad in the UK, you will probably be restricted in Europe, usually to around 25GB.

The UK government has passed a law of a £45 limit for phone charges in any one trip, meaning that's the most you will ever be charged (without approving more). Should you hit that limit, you'll receive a text asking if you want to keep using your phone abroad.

If you say yes, your charges will keep growing. If you say no, you won't be able to make calls, texts or use the internet. If you feel you’ll be using your phone a lot, make sure you have an overseas package or use a network which won't charge for roaming or making overseas calls.

If you're going on a longer trip, you may prefer to buy a SIM card for the country(ies) you are travelling in. You can often buy these at service stations, big supermarkets and in towns/ cities. As long as your phone is unlocked, you should be able to pop it in, register if required, add credit and off you go.

Of course, while that SIM card is in your phone, you won’t be able to see or receive calls or texts to your usual number, so a cheap second-hand phone might be a good idea for a longer trip.

Getting Online / Wi-Fi

Both my husband and I work from the road. Decent internet access is ESSENTIAL for us. 90% of my website and Youtube Channel (and this book!) have been created using mobile data whilst travelling.

There are several ways to get internet or mobile Wi-Fi in your camper as you tour. What is acceptable for you will depend entirely on if you just enjoy browsing Facebook for fun, want to Zoom with family or if you need stable connections for work.

Assuming you want internet in your van, and don't want to find a cafe with Wi-Fi (McDonalds are always a good bet!), these are the main options available to you:

- Use a Phone / iPad with a SIM card and data connection/ hot spot (most phones have this now).
- Buy a Wi-Fi dongle.
- Install a specialist system / satellite internet on your motorhome.

Don't panic if this sounds difficult. Let's look at the options for mobile Wi-Fi in more detail.

Using a phone for internet

On MOST recent smartphone contracts, your mobile phone probably is already set up to use data (not always the case for Pay-as-you-go tariffs.) If it is, and you have a 3G phone signal or better (4G/5G), you should be able to connect to the internet on your phone, which allows you to check emails/ Facebook etc.

You can **also use your mobile phone as a Wi-Fi hotspot**; meaning that other devices which DON'T have their own SIM card, (like a laptop, Kindle or possibly an iPad), can connect to your phone via a personal hotspot and use that data.

Mobile Wi-Fi: how to set up a personal hotspot using your phone

On an iPhone, you can find your personal hotspot in the settings menu and follow the guidelines. Name it something easily recognisable (like “Kat's phone”) and SET A PASSWORD, you don't want everyone else in the campsite logging onto your phone and using up all your data!
On the device you want to use (i.e. the laptop or Kindle), go to the Wi-Fi / network selection and find your phone's name in the options. Select it, input the password and you'll be connected!
As long as you have a phone signal and mobile data, it should work fine (might be sow, but will work.)

Of course, don't forget that this will use your phone's data allowance (usually 25GB when roaming), so be careful what you do using it or you'll reach your limit fast.

Things like using maps, watching TV, streaming videos and browsing Instagram reels can all use up a LOT of data very quickly.

How to use a Wi-Fi dongle

For this reason, we chose to get a Wi-Fi dongle to use in our motorhome. We use one on EE and, as long as there is a phone signal, we've been able to get pretty decent internet.

I should point out, we're used to living-on-a-boat internet, NOT high-speed fibre broadband. A Wi-Fi dongle will be much slower than high-speed home internet.

However, most of my website has been built using the motorhome Wi-Fi dongle, my husband manages his business using it, and I'm using it right now to edit this book, so it works well enough for us.

Over the years, both on the boats and in the vans, we've used several different dongles. They're fairly easy to set up and all work much the same way.

You need to buy a dongle and a data SIM card on a network to use with it. Ideally, get a network different to your phone, so you increase the chance of one of them having signal.

Prepaid data sims are great, but read the small print; often, once they're activated, you only have a certain length of time to use the data before you lose it.

We pay for ours monthly because we use it so much- Pay-as-you-go was too expensive.

Do whatever works best for you, but make sure it is data which can be used abroad in Europe.

TOP TIP: Make sure you buy the correct size SIM card for the dongle. Most take either nano-SIMs or micro-SIMs; no, they're not the same. If in doubt, go into a mobile shop and ask for advice once you have the dongle.

If you don't use the dongle for a long period of time (I think it's around 6 months) you might have to reactivate before you can use it again- this should be mentioned in your instructions.

Which mobile data network works best in Europe?

We have devices on several different UK networks; 3, Vodafone and the Wi-Fi dongle is on EE.

When we're travelling in Europe, there is a definite difference between which networks can pick up signals best in different spots. For example, in the French Alps at the Mont Blanc aire,

I couldn't get a signal on my 3 phone at all, but Mr WB got a great one on Vodafone, so we used his phone as a hotspot. There's no right answer to which is 'best', but EE and o2 have the best coverage maps.

How many devices can you connect to a motorhome Wi-Fi dongle?

We often have 7 devices connected to one dongle. Two laptops, two iPads and three phones. And that's without Jade being in the camper.

Most people won't need that many devices, but it shows it can handle it! Some dongles have a limit on how many devices can be connected, so check before you buy if like us you have a lot of devices to use at once.

Want to know what we use? You can find everything you need at **wandering-bird.com/gear or scan here >>>>>**

How to get internet in the middle of nowhere

But what if there isn't a phone signal? Are there any options to get internet?
Some of our favourite nights in the motorhome have been when we haven't had internet. Like the night we spent up the Swiss Alps under the Milky Way, planning how to change our lives. Don't be scared of not having a phone/ Wi-Fi signal for the odd night- it's oddly liberating, even with teenagers.

However, as two people who work from the road, we know how important staying in touch can be. The only way to get an internet signal if there are no phone signals is by satellite. It can be done- but it is expensive and VERY slow.

We used to use a satellite phone for internet when we were sailing; that was painful and expensive enough for us not to bother with it on the road! Instead, we plan our trips up mountains (which is usually when we struggle with network coverage) for weekends or days when it doesn't matter if we're out of comms for a while.

Motorhome Wi-Fi internet booster

A Wi-Fi booster is an aerial or small box which is fixed to the roof of your motorhome/ camper and boosts any Wi-Fi signal it receives, allowing you to get a better connection.

NOTE: It BOOSTS an existing signal. It can't magic one out of thin air. Trust me, we tried.

We've used a booster on the boat for years and now have an aerial permanently fixed to the motorhome roof. It definitely helps. Just be mindful of height and going over 3m tall, you might wish to get a removable one to reduce toll costs.

Try to get a system which can be powered by either 12v or 240v, that way you can use it to boost a campsite Wi-Fi or while wild parking.

Using a TV in Europe

The main ways to watch TV in your motorhome, campervan or caravan are:

- Digital TV
- Satellite TV
- Online / catchup using apps / internet

We don't have a proper TV in our motorhome at all, we use our laptops or iPads to stream whatever we want to watch. I should point out that we aren't big TV watchers and it tends to be mostly sport we watch live. For movies or shows we watch on either Netflix, iTunes or Amazon Prime.

It used to be the case that you could stream UK TV programmes pretty much anywhere in Europe, using a system like Sky Go or one of the catchup apps.

Sadly, this is another casualty of BREXIT and it's a lot harder now as much of UK tv is blocked to within the UK only.
However, there is a way around this and that's to use a VPN. We've used one called Express VPN with great success. You do need to pay for it but it's well worth it. I have it set up on my phone and iPad so I can watch things like F1 or the Tour de France on catch up apps.

Dedicated Motorhome TVs

Most motorhome / caravan TVs are 12v and they are infinitely better at power management than normal household TVs, making them much more efficient.

Also, a motorhome TV is designed to be moved around, so it's more robust than a home TV, which is designed to stay in one place for most of its life. A motorhome TV is designed to withstand the vibrations which come from being driven all over the place, not to mention the jolts and bumps from even the most careful driver.

Lastly, most household TVs weigh more than a motorhome TV. Sure, some of that is down to size, but it's also down to how they're designed, which helps keep you within your motorhome payload limits.

Unless you plan to ONLY ever watch a TV when you are plugged into mains in a campsite, you'll need a 12v TV, which will run off your motorhome leisure battery. Without the 12v capability, you can only use a 230v plug (like the one in your house), which of course only works when you are plugged into the mains system.
I guess you could run it off a generator too, but you'd need a big generator and it would be pretty noisy!

If you're planning to travel to Europe with your motorhome and want to watch UK TV, you will need a satellite or online system - Terrestrial digital television (DVB-T) won't work.

Satellite digital television (DVB-S)

You can get hundreds of television and radio stations which include BBC, ITV stations, SKY News (depending on package), CNN, Film 4 and many others using satellite television. These are often called “Freesat” channels. You can buy televisions with Freesat already built in, so you do not need to buy a separate box with these TVs, but you will still need a satellite aerial.

NOTE: An aerial is most likely to be some sort of ‘satellite dish', either permanently fixed to the roof or manual.
You also need a receiver to watch satellite tv. The most well-known one in the UK is the Sky ‘Digibox' but others are available. Usually, along with purchasing the receiver, if you want to watch premium channels, you need to buy a monthly/ annual subscription (such as to Sky).

NOTE: Sky viewing cards cannot be moved from one digibox to another. You either need to take your digibox from the house with you in the motorhome/ caravan OR get two boxes and viewing cards. Also, Sky's Ts & Cs state that the box cannot be taken abroad.

They have another subscription option (or they did last time I checked!) called Sky Go. We used to use this around Europe to watch essential programmes (like Game of Thrones). To do this we needed to use a VPN to say that we were in the UK.

There are also services like Now TV which you watch online and give you access to Sky channels as part of their monthly package. Again, you'll probably need a VPN to use it properly.

Internet TV

As I mentioned before, we haven't had a TV in our motorhome for years. We rarely watch TV 'live' and tend to watch catch up channels instead.

Also, we realised that to get UK TV in Europe, we either needed an expensive and heavy satellite system, or find a way to watch on the internet.

So now we only ever watch TV on our laptops or iPads and access UK catch-up apps such as BBC iPlayer from all over the world, using a VPN. **We have used Express VPN without problem for years.**

NOTE: We continue to pay for a UK TV licence. We still have one registered on the same address where our mail goes, which covers us for use when we are back in the UK and also when abroad.
Obviously, in order to watch TV online, you will need internet. You can either use the 3G/4G which is on your phone/ iPad (you can use it as a hotspot for a laptop) OR you can connect it to a Wi-Fi dongle.

Another option is to use a 'stick' which plugs into a laptop or even a TV and gives you TV that way. Two of the most popular are the Amazon Firestick, and the Roku stick. Again, you will need a Wi-Fi/ internet connection for either of these to work.

If you're not living in your van full-time and want to avoid high data bills, remember to download some movies / tv shows to your device before you leave the UK.

TOP TIP: Start playing each download (the first 3-4 seconds) whilst in the UK, and then you shouldn't need a VPN to watch the rest as long as you turn your device to airplane mode before you start watching.

Food in Europe

I've seen some people get so concerned about food in Europe, so I'm here to ease your concerns- people eat food in Europe too! ;)

You'll find plenty of supermarkets and shops all over the place. Having said that, if you have a dietary condition or are travelling with a picky eater, Europe can be tougher, so here are some tips for you to make life easier.

Pack some easy food to prepare for the first night. We're big believers in eating local food. It's one of our favourite parts about travelling BUT when you've been driving all day and all you've seen are service stations, something easy, satisfying and familiar is a great comfort as you settle in on your epic adventure. You might not win any culinary or health awards, but your sanity might just be saved!!

Of course, this is harder now we can't bring meat from the UK, so **prepare to stop en-route for supplies** on day one. Remember, if you're travelling by ferry, you will need to have the fridge turned off, so DON'T stock up before you leave the UK as it will probably go bad before you can use it.

Lidl and Aldi have stores all over Europe and they're great. We love shopping at local markets and shops, but if you want basic foods at a decent price, you can't go wrong with either of them. They also have large car parks, which are usually easy to get a motorhome into/ out of.

You won't always find the same brands or exact foods as you get in the UK (can't find custard creams, Jaffa cakes or Dairy Milk anywhere) but there will usually be some substitute to keep you going.

If you do have dietary concerns, be sure to note what these are in the language of the country(ies) you're visiting and you may prefer to cook more than you eat out, especially if you're travelling in more rural areas, another good advantage to having a kitchen on wheels!

Travelling with Kids

We love road trips with our daughter; she's a lot of fun and we love seeing the world through her eyes, but there have certainly been trips in the past when she was younger which were HARD work.

However, don't be deterred. I feel like we spend some of our best times together in the van and things are (usually!) a lot less stressed than they are on a normal car journey, especially if you're prepared.

Here are some tips for travelling with young (or teenage!) children:

Accept that kids are NOT going to be as excited by the amazing scenery as you are. Give them something to do. Jade's preferred past-time is listening to music, but she also enjoys reading or drawing.

We never let her have pens / crayons in the car when she was little (as she'd drop them and then cry!) but as a teenager she's usually better at managing her stuff, (although she now finds drawing makes her car sick.) She's also not allowed any drinks not in a sealed thermos flask, as they always seem to spill! Putting cup holders / netting bags next to their seats is a great idea.

Try not to put things where kids can see them but can't get to them- this will only lead to tantrums. Give them a few things to play with and hide everything else. You can change the toys at each rest stop as a reward.

A lot of these activities will depend on the age of your little (or big!) ones. From about 12, Jade would sit quietly with her headphones on, listening to music she'd downloaded and watching the world pass as we drove. The only meltdowns came when she realised she was out of battery and/or Wi-Fi.
TOP TIP: Make sure your kids charge EVERYTHING before you leave - phones, earbuds, iPads... everything. Packing a pair of wired headphones is a good idea too.

Plan breaks in advance – ideally somewhere with a park for them to let off some steam. If they know how far they have to go between stops, it can help them mentally prepare. Just add some extra time in case you run into traffic.

Car games help to keep everyone occupied on a long trip, as does talking about things you're going to see / do on arrival. Keeping some snacks to hand helps too.

Whilst we're on the subject of food, many kids won't share your excitement for the local cuisine. Most kids, including ours, like to eat something familiar, especially when everything else is different.
So, in order to make life easier and less stressful for all of you, try to make sure there is food on board you know your kids will eat, rather than turning your holiday into a battle of wills.

Little things like this make a road trip far more fun for all the family!

Travelling with Dogs

Kids, dogs…there's not a whole lot of difference… 😆
We've made several mistakes when travelling with our dog. We got him as a puppy and he grew up in the motorhome, but even with this great start it's not been all smooth sailing.

Mac and I in Monaco

Here are some tips for travelling with a dog:

Create them a little space of their own, especially if you have young kids. Dogs need a time out zone where they can relax and sleep. Adult dogs need around 17 hours of sleep a day, and puppies need even more! *(Anyone else want to come back as a dog...!)*
Mac has a mat which is HIS mat. We move it around the van to suit us (this isn't always the best option) but he adapts and curls up on it wherever it is. We tried to create

a cubby hole under a seat- but he prefers being able to see out of a window when he wants to.

Dogs MUST be restrained in the vehicle when you're driving as they cannot wander around loose or you risk being stopped and fined by police (not to mention it's dangerous in the event of an accident).

Mac travelled in a crate for a long time. Initially it was a fabric crate... until he learned how to scratch his way through it! Now he is older, we use a harness and a seat-belt restraint and he sits on a seat in the dinette so he can see out of the window. Some people put fixed points on the floor to keep their dogs still and safe.

Make sure they have access to water and get lots of rest breaks. Also, be sure to keep them cool on hot days and NEVER leave them in a vehicle unattended on a warm day.

If your dog is new to motorhomes, treat them as you would a scared child. Most dogs are anxious about change and a motorhome makes some weird noises, especially in the back. Clicks, bangs and other things will worry them, not helped by you sitting up front, further away than usual. Do lots of short journeys with fun walks at the end to get them used to it.

Dogs are usually allowed on most campsites unless there are local wildlife restrictions (check in advance). They are usually required to be on a lead unless in a dog walking area. Make sure your dog is restrained at your pitch and can't wander into the next person's bay.... *Not that WE have EVER done this *cough cough** (sorry neighbour)

We do leave Mac alone occasionally on a campsite or aire whilst we go shopping. We never leave him for longer than 2 hours and NEVER when the weather is warm- vans warm up just like cars do and can get dangerously hot in a very short time.

Mac is also not a 'barker'. If you have a dog who misses you and likes to make a lot of noise while you're gone- expect to be reported to the campsite by annoyed neighbours.

If you want to take your dog on public transport in Europe (where allowed), you will need a muzzle and to carry their pet passport.

Yes, having a dog with you on your travels can stop you doing things; we can rarely visit a museum or castle together. But he's part of the family and an awesome road trip buddy and we love having him with us, so it's worth the compromise for us. For shorter trips, you might prefer to leave your dog behind so you have more freedom.
More and more people are now travelling with cats and other animals. Please check with your vet about requirements needed to cross the border and use common sense when leaving them inside the vehicle, especially during hot weather.

Staying Safe on the Road

Another important section and something which worries many people, including me. After all, no-one likes to feel vulnerable or targeted.

One of the biggest concerns is when wild camping and I'm not going to lie- a motorhome parked in the middle of nowhere on its own is potentially more vulnerable than a motorhome on a campsite.

Having said that, in some ways I think it can be safer. Let me explain why.

There are two types of theft- premeditated and opportunistic. Generally, premeditated is carried out by 'professional' thieves, who tend to have proper equipment to overcome locks, trackers, etc etc.
And those people like to plan.

They know the easiest campsites to access and the best places to watch for vulnerable vehicles. Which makes campsites or aires their preferred target as they know the lay of the land. You also have to worry about other people on the campsite who may not be as upstanding as you are.

In contrast, when you wild camp, NO ONE KNOWS WHERE YOU ARE. So the only threat you have is from opportunists passing-by, who are often looking for easy and quick targets. You'd have to be really unlucky to get targeted if you're staying somewhere remote and well away from built-up areas.

Opportunists are mostly scared off by a few simple tactics, such as large signs in the window stating the vehicle is covered by CCTV (even if it's not) or security devices like steering wheel locks.

We do actually use a camera system in our motorhome while travelling and it's brilliant for letting us check on the van if we go out.

It also lets us know our dog is ok if we leave him alone for an hour or two. **You can see it here or at wandering-bird.com/gear >>>**

Another good deterrent is 'Beware of the Dog' signs.

You can upgrade motorhome door locks and even window locks. There are plenty of options on the market. Lastly, keep something hard and heavy to hand. It's not illegal to defend yourself and you are totally allowed to grab an object which happens to be nearby- like a crowbar or a baseball bat.

(According to a lawyer friend of ours, you MUST carry a tennis ball in the motorhome if you have a bat- otherwise it counts as a weapon. But it's totally fine to leave it to hand overnight.)

We also try to avoid places which could be riskier. Motorway services are a good example of this- there are many reports of people staying overnight in their vehicles and having problems, so we never stay there.

We also choose not to wild camp or use aires close to big cities, ferry ports or the Tunnel, as they are renowned for attracting troublemakers and thieves.

TOP TIP: Keep yourself safe. Don’t post your location on Instagram or social media until after you’ve left. You never know who might be watching.

What to Do in the Event of an Accident

In the event of a road traffic accident, you'll need the European Claim Form which should have been provided by your insurer before you leave. All parties complete and sign the form at the scene and then send a copy to your insurer for assessment.

What to do at the scene:

- Stop your vehicle immediately but safely- out of the flow of traffic if possible.
- If a vehicle is blocking the road, use hazard lights and put the red warning triangle 30 metres from the scene to warn approaching traffic.
- Don your hi-vis jacket (applies for passengers too).
- Exchange your details with the other involved parties. Be sure to get: Name and address of all the people involved in the accident; Vehicle registration numbers of all parties; Insurance company details of all parties.
- Take photos of damage using a camera, GoPro or phone.

Do NOT sign any forms unless you understand completely what you are signing. Once you've signed, it's legally binding.

Power Management

Power management is essential to nearly all motorhome owners, especially if you're going to be staying off grid.

Let's walk through the basics first.

First and most important thing; when you are not plugged in to electricity and don't have a generator/ inverter running, **you CANNOT use your normal 230v plugs on your motorhome.**

That means your lovely electric kettle, toaster, hairdryer and everything else won't work while you're not plugged into mains. At all.

Therefore, to get power, you have two options; buy and run a generator big enough to power those devices (but probably not at once!) OR find alternative solutions.
We actually carry a generator and we've used it a handful of times. I always said I never wanted to be 'that van' which turns up and ruins a beautiful spot with nasty noise but, in an emergency, we've been grateful to have it.
Our preferred power-management option is to create systems which work off-grid.

- We have a gas kettle.
- We don't have a toaster- we use the grill (which is nowhere near as good for toast but better than nothing.)

- We have LED lights inside the motorhome which saves power.
- We fitted a solar panel which helps recharge both the leisure and engine battery.
- We have power-banks to recharge laptops and phones.

Hair-Drying

Hair-Drying is a pain without electric. I have yet to find a 12v one which is any good. I tried a battery one once and that wasn't great either.

In warm climates, I let it air dry but in colder regions I use dry shampoo a LOT and we have been known to run the generator for 15 minutes in a morning whilst I dry my hair.

Get a low watt hairdryer- mine is 800w and does the job fairly well on my long, thick hair.

If you're going to be wild camping and staying without power a lot, there are many more tips in our Wild Camping eBook- get it for a discount here or at wandering-bird.com/wild **>>>>>**

How do we charge electronics?

Managing your power is essential if you're not using campsites daily. Our trick is to charge EVERYTHING while we drive.
It's very rare that we stay anywhere longer than 2 nights, so we drive pretty frequently. During that time, we will charge:

- 4 phones (12v sockets in front of motorhome, we bought double adaptors for the cigarette lighters so we can fit them all in.)
- 2 iPads (using 12v sockets again).
- Sat Nav
- 2 laptops using our inverter, which runs off the engine battery.
- 3 x drone batteries if they need it, using the inverter and an extension lead.
- Camera batteries for my DSLR, again using the power lead from the inverter.

Yeah, we have a lot of electronics and that's not even including our daughter's kit if she's travelling with us!
On our last motorhome, we had a second leisure battery, which helped with our power demand. However, we also had an electric bed, which was incredibly power-hungry.

In our new motorhome, we only have one 110amp leisure battery and so far feel no need to get a second one. Make sure your leisure battery is a good size and is looked after during the winter- cold can completely destroy a battery.

NOTE: If there is no space for a second battery, you shouldn't fit one unless you get it done professionally- it can invalidate your insurance and/ or warranty.

How to choose an inverter

An inverter is one of the essential things we use on our motorhome. In very simple terms, it allows you to use the power from your battery (12v) to power 230v appliances.

Choosing one is simple... once you know how. Get one too big and it will damage your battery. Too small and it won't be able to power your appliances.

As a (very!) rough guide, a 1000w inverter will use 100amps/ hour. If your leisure battery is only 100amps, it will drain very quickly- and batteries rarely recover if they are completely discharged, which means you can only run the inverter for around 30 minutes- probably not long enough to charge everything.

So you need one which won't drain your battery too quickly. With a 100Amp battery, I'd suggest around 500w should be fine.

We keep our inverter connected to the battery, but only turn it on when the motorhome engine is running (and has been running for about 20 minutes to give the other battery time to charge.) This system has worked well for us so far for charging electronics as we drive.

Motorhoming in Norway with our second van

Motorhoming in Winter

Many people choose to close up their vans for the winter and that's fine ***(if you'd like some advice on how to do this, head to wandering-bird.com and search 'winter'.)***

However, some of us use our vans all year. If you're planning to travel to Europe in winter, there are some things you need to know.

Of course, there are two main reasons people head to Europe during winter- either chasing the snow or chasing the sun.

Chasing the Sun

If you're chasing the sun (i.e.- heading as far south as possible), there's not a whole lot you need to do differently, with the exception of needing winter tyres / snow chains (see below) and possibly some other gear 'just in case'.

But, once you're down in the warmth, you'll use your motorhome much like any other time.

Campsites / Aires

Be aware that many campsites either close or get booked up far in advance, especially if they're near the beach. Aires usually stay open all year but can be closed due to maintenance (which is why an app is better).

Chasing the Snow

If you're chasing the snow and want to head to the slopes with your motorhome or campervan, the first thing to tell you is that you're not as crazy as you fear you are! Plenty of Europeans go 'motorhome skiing' and there is infrastructure in place to support it.

Still, it's important to remember that how you use your motorhome between Spring-Autumn will not be the same as using it in the middle of winter up a mountain in -17c! Your systems will not function in the way you might be used to, and there will be other jobs you need to do to keep everything running.

Waste Tanks

When you park up, place an external bucket or container under the grey waste drain, and leave it open. This helps prevent freezing. Be sure to empty the bucket regularly! Most Aires will have places to dispose of waste, at least some of the time.

Water

Many aires and campsites will leave a freshwater tap running constantly so that it doesn't freeze. Don’t turn it off.

Winter Tyres

As already mentioned in this guide, many countries insist on winter tyres and the carrying of snow chains, especially in mountainous regions but usually you’ll need them for everywhere within that country.

In November 2021, France introduced a new law in many of their mountainous regions (48 in total) where you MUST either have proper winter tyres fitted (with the mountain logo) OR carry snow chains / snow socks.

They also allow studded tyres, even though these are banned in almost every other country in Europe.

You can use 4-season tyres, but you’ll need snow chains as well.

Other Gear

As well as winter tyres and snow chains, you'll probably find it useful to have the following:

- Decent snow shovel.
- Mud-mats
- Generator
- Long handled brush.
- Thermal screen
- Skirting around bottom of van.
- Collapsible bucket for waste water.
- Window vac for condensation.

Campsites / Aires

Many campsites away from the mountains close after the end of peak season (around end of September). Some stay open until the end of October but relatively few are open all year. For this reason, it's important to choose and book your campsite as far in advance as possible, especially if you're going to a popular ski resort.

Many aires in mountainous regions are closed due to snowfall. Also, you might find the water turned off to avoid frost damage, even if you can still park there.
One of the best resources for checking winter stopovers is snomadsites.com

Insulation

If you are planning on heading to the mountains during winter, you'll probably need to add insulation to your motorhome, including lagging pipes inside and out.
This is especially important if you're planning to stay up in the mountains for several days, as the pipes will freeze and you'll be left without water.

Extra carpets/ rugs on the floor helps insulate the inside too.

Heating

Even if you're chasing the sunshine down in Spain, it can still get cold enough to need heating during winter and in the mountains it's essential.

Many campsites in the mountains don't have 16-amp electricity supply and so your electric heating might not work as well as you are used to. It also means you need to be selective about how much electricity you are using at once (you don't want to be THAT van which is constantly tripping everyone's electric…!)
Gas heating works well, but you will use a lot of it; we use around 6kg every 2 days.
Diesel heating is a great alternative, but many vans don't come with it as standard. If you do fit it, be aware of the weight and how it affects your motorhome payload. Another option is an oil-filled radiator, but make sure it's low wattage.

Whilst on the subject of staying warm, invest in thermal layers (for you) and a nice thick 15 tog duvet for the bed. You can also get 12v electric blankets & bring hot water bottles!

Wet Clothing

You'll need a plan for wet shoes / boots / coats / ski gear. Where will you put them when you enter the van to avoid getting mud/ snow all over the place?
Don't forget, you'll also need somewhere to dry wet gear. It helps if you have a bathroom with a heating vent, like on our Swift- you can string a line across the top and hang everything up to dry overnight.

Condensation

One of the biggest problems of winter motorhoming is dealing with condensation and damp. It's impossible to avoid it completely, but there are some things you can do to reduce the effect it has on you.
Damp / wet clothing is a huge culprit. If the campsite has a drying room for wet ski gear, use it.
Also, this is the time to use a laundrette and a dryer if you don't normally, drying a load of wet clothes in a damp van is miserable.
Despite the cold, your van will benefit from a little ventilation, so try to open a window at least once a day for some fresh air.

Some people run a dehumidifier, but you might struggle with electricity for that. Non-electric damp boxes or pouches (like the ones you put in wardrobes) are a good idea to soak up at least some of the moisture in the air. And a good window vac is the best thing you'll ever buy!

Solar

You can't rely on solar power during winter to recharge your batteries in the same way you can at other times of the year. The sun isn't as strong, there are more hours of darkness and more areas of shade. Also, you'll be using more power than you might normally.

If you already have a solar panel fitted, then by all means use what you can, but don't rely on it as your only power source.

Battery

Batteries do not like cold. They don't run as effectively so you need to be more vigilant about looking after them, making sure they don't run too low, giving them a good charge regularly and generally babying them.

LED lights

We always recommend LED lights to save power, especially if you're staying off-grid a lot, but in winter it becomes essential as 'normal' bulbs drain the power too quickly.

Country Guides

In this section, I've highlighted some of the most important rules for the most popular countries in Europe, along with fun places to visit and itinerary ideas for you.

FRANCE

Useful things to know

Emergency Numbers: 112 will get you everything
Language: French and some local dialects, like Breton. English is usually spoken in campsites and tourist areas, but not often elsewhere.
Currency: Euro
Cards: most major credit and debit cards are accepted. American Express is occasionally accepted in large stores (but not at tolls and often not at fuel stations).
Time zone: GMT+1 (or always one hour ahead in BST).
Mobile Phone and Internet: It's usually possible to use your UK phone and data in France but do check with your provider.
Tipping: Tipping is not customary, but always appreciated. 10-15% in upscale restaurants is acceptable.
Shops: Food prices are pretty inexpensive. Many shops close on Sundays. Bigger supermarkets may be open but close at lunchtime. If bakeries open on Sundays, they are often closed on Mondays instead. Many shops and

businesses also shut for a long lunch (between 12-2pm) and some will not open on Wednesday afternoons.

Where to Go

If you enjoy motorhoming in the UK, you're going to LOVE touring in France. There's everything you could want, from fantastic campsites on the beach, vineyards, incredible history and plenty of places to explore.
Here are a few ideas for some of the places you can visit on your France road trip.

Northern France

Many people drive through northern France as a way of getting somewhere else, but there is a lot to discover here.

Some of our favourite places include:

- The Normandy beaches. Everyone should do this at least once.
- Mont St Michel- one of the most historical places in France.
- Brittany
- The Loire Valley. If you like chateaux and history, this is for you!
- Ile de Re and La Rochelle
- Strasbourg- one of the prettiest cities in France.

On a side note, I know Paris is in the north of France and we LOVE Paris... but not with a motorhome or camper.

Park up in a campsite nearby and travel in by public transport or taxi. Driving in Paris is a law unto itself!

Southern France

Some of our favourite places in the south of France include:

- The Gorges du Verdon. One of the most spectacular places we have EVER been with our motorhome.
- The Pyrenees, especially the Cirque du Gavarnie. It's jaw-droppingly beautiful.
- French Alps. Exploring the Alps with a motorhome is awesome. We also love Lake Annecy and you MUST do the cable car up Mont Blanc.

  Biarritz, Bordeaux and the Dune du Pilat- make sure you allow time to visit some of the incredible vineyards in the area!

When to Go

The best time to visit France is whenever you have time to explore! Some people pop over on the Eurotunnel for a weekend break. Others take a month to explore one corner.

The beauty of France being so large is that usually there will be an area with decent weather. And the beauty of exploring with a home on wheels is that you can drive to wherever the weather is best for you.

Generally, the best weather is between April - October. You may still get decent temperatures into November on the French Riviera (that's the coast on the Med, not the Atlantic coast.) If you're planning to go skiing in France, then December - March are your best times.

France has recently passed a new law, insisting you have either winter tyres fitted or carry snow chains / snow socks if visiting mountainous regions between 01 November and 31 March; see gear section.

It can get VERY hot in summer, especially down south. It can also be amazingly windy- you'll find many cafes and restaurants near the Mediterranean or Atlantic bolt down their outdoor furniture.

Our favourite times are Spring and Autumn. It's usually warm, especially in the south, but there aren't huge crowds and it's easy to get access to popular tourist places.

Driving in France

French drivers are generally not too bad (at least, not compared to Italy!) The scariest thing about drivers in France are the *(how do I put this politely?!)* older generation who don't realise that priorité à droite is no longer a thing!

Some quick tips for driving in France:

- France drives on the right, like much of Europe.

- The road system is set up for you driving on the right. Signs are on that side, roundabouts have helpful arrows and slip roads are pointed the right way. I promise, it's not as hard as it sounds.
- The maximum speed for private vehicles under 3.5t is 130kph (81mph) on motorways but speed limits are lower for cars towing caravans and for motorhomes over 3.5t in weight.
- If driving through towns and villages, only use the horn in an emergency.
- Buses and trams have right of way.
- Seatbelts are compulsory.
- In-car speed camera detectors and motorhome sat-nav systems warning of the presence of radars are illegal (whether they're in use or not!)
- Using a mobile phone while driving is illegal, but you can use a hands-free unit without earbuds.
- Minor traffic offences can result in on-the-spot fines.
- UK driving licences are perfectly acceptable to use.

Petrol and Diesel

Petrol and diesel are widely available. Many fuel stations are 24h on the main roads and are self-service with card machines. Diesel is diesel or gazole.

Many people worry whether they should fill up in UK or France. In our experience, France is often a little cheaper, BUT there are often fuel strikes, especially in summer. We ALWAYS fill up in the UK before we go... just in case.

Priorité à droite in France

France no longer has the old 'priorité à droite' rule, (which meant you had to stop ON the roundabout for anyone coming onto it!)

HOWEVER, expect the occasional older French resident to merrily sail onto the roundabout and expect you to stop for them. Also, I believe it still exists in some special places in France- like the Arc de Triomphe.

Tolls in France

France, like nearly all countries in Europe which don't have a vignette system, has tolls on its major roads. You collect a ticket at the machine as you enter the road system and pay (either a person or machine) at the end in cash or on a card.

Tolls in France are some of the most expensive in Europe (but not as bad as Norway!)

Depending on your route and height of your motorhome, a trip from Northern France to the south will cost around 50€. If your motorhome is over 3m high, you will be charged as a Class 4 vehicle, not class 2, so it could be as much as 90€.

Most motorhomes are calculated for class B, regardless of the number of axles. You can use a tollpass / telepass (like e-Movis) or you can pay-as-you-go by cash or card (we always recommend carrying some cash- just in case!) Signs show the means of payment accepted in each lane.

Speed Limits in France

Speed Limits are as follows (unless otherwise signed!)

- 130 km/h (80 mph) on motorways
- 110km/hr (69mph) on major roads
- 90 km/h (56 mph) on minor roads out of town
- 50 km/h (31 mph) in built-up areas

In rain or snow conditions, the limit is lowered to 110 k/h on motorways and 90 k/h on trunk roads- this WILL NOT be signposted- you're expected to know it

Motorhomes with trailers or caravans:

- motorways 80 km/h (50 mph)
- major out-of-town roads 70 km/h (44 mph)
- minor out-of-town roads 70 km/h (44 mph)
- built-up areas- 50 km/h (31 mph)
-

Motorhomes and Campervans weighing over 3.5 tonnes and under 12 tonnes:

- motorways 100 km/h (62 mph)
- major out-of-town roads 80 km/h (50 mph)
- minor out-of-town roads 80 km/h (50 mph)
- urban areas 50 km/h (31 mph)

Speed Cameras in France

If you see a sign for a speed camera, there's nearly always a camera within a mile- often hidden near a bridge.

Beware of parked cars on the sides of fast roads. Entrapment is allowed in France and police will regularly park an old car at the side of the road with a hidden camera in it, and then they'll pull you over further down and give you a speeding ticket, which must be paid in cash on the spot- or you'll be escorted to a cash machine and asked to withdraw the fine.

They've also just started privatising cars to carry speeding equipment- meaning anyone can be paid to have the gear in their vehicle… with no warning whatsoever.

SPAIN

Useful things to know

Emergency Numbers: 112 will get you everything
Language: There are several local variations of Spanish. Castilian is most common, but there is also Basque, Catalan and some smaller dialects. English usually spoken in campsites and in tourist areas, but not often elsewhere..
Currency: Euro
Cards: most major credit and debit cards are accepted. American Express is only taken in large stores (not at tolls and often not at fuel stations).
Time zone: GMT+1 (or one hour ahead in BST).
Mobile Phone and Internet: It's usually possible to use your UK phone and data in Spain, but do check with your provider. If not, 1p Mobile SIM cards are widely available and a cheap option for phone calls.

Tipping: Tipping is not customary, but always appreciated. If you do tip, remember servers probably won't get anything added to a card payment, so try to use cash where possible. 10-15% in upscale restaurants is acceptable

Shops: Food prices are not expensive. Many shops close on Sundays. Many shops and businesses also shut for a long lunch (between 12-2pm) and some will not open on Wednesday afternoons.

Visiting Spain

When you think of Spain, many people think of overcrowded beaches in Benidorm, drunken teenagers and possibly Sangria. But I promise you, there is much more to Spain than the Costa del Sol, especially if you're travelling and touring in a motorhome or campervan.

The landscape changes from the rugged north, with mountains and scenic views to rival anywhere else in Europe, to desert and arid areas, down to the sparkling azure blue of the Mediterranean. There is history and culture everywhere you look, as well as friendly and welcoming people, delicious food and SUNSHINE- even in winter.

Where to Go in Spain

When planning a tour of Spain, the first thing you need to do is to figure out where you're going (and how long you have for your road trip!)

If you're driving from the UK to Spain, you need to allow the time it will take to drive through France to Spain (and back again!)

Of course, if you only have a week break, then you'll only have a few days to explore the country and the further south you go, the less exploring time you have. On the other hand, if you have 10-14 days or longer, you can get a lot further south, certainly as far as Andalucia and possibly even further if you're happy to drive every day.

Touring Spain in Winter

In our opinion, southern Spain is the perfect European winter destination. It's a lot warmer than the UK- and there's nothing like a little sunshine to chase away those January blues. Average temperatures in Malaga are 17°c (but only 12°c in Madrid- that extra bit south does make a big difference.)

In the past, Southern Spain has been VERY crowded during the winter months- many Northern Europeans (like us Brits!) head to get some winter sunshine. However, now that BREXIT has happened and rules have changed, you might find things a little quieter, certainly with British vans.

Northern Spain is mountainous and you can expect snow during winter- it will be cold, even on sunny days. If you're planning to stay to the north, you'll need to bring warm clothing.

Other times of the year in Spain

Summer

Of course, Spain is a classic summer destination and can be crowded, especially along the Mediterranean coast. For us, we find it too hot during high summer, especially as we travel with a dog and keeping a dog cool is never easy (especially if they're a cocker spaniel who doesn't understand the meaning of the word 'chill'.)

If you are going to be travelling to Spain during summer, we highly recommend you have an awning, you'll definitely need the shade and protection from the sun. You'll probably also want some form of air conditioning or at least a fan in your camper- temperatures can get up to 40+°c regularly.

Spring and Autumn

The best times to visit are probably the shoulder seasons of Spring and Autumn. Temperatures are still warm enough to enjoy the beaches and swimming in the sea, but there are much fewer tourists and you will be able to find motorhome parking without booking in advance.

Planning a route from the UK to Spain

For some reason, driving from the UK to Spain seems to confuse people more than any other country. Perhaps it's because there are several options, or perhaps because there's a mountain range in the way, but it's something which gets asked over and over again. There are a couple of options to choose from:

Ferry or driving from UK to Spain?

The first question to ask yourself is whether you want to drive from the UK through France and down to Spain, or whether you want to take the ferry from the UK directly to the north Spanish coast.

Generally, taking a ferry from the UK to Spain is much more expensive than driving through France (depending on time of year and type of cabin), but it does save you having to do all the driving yourself.

Ferry with a motorhome direct to Spain

You can travel with Brittany Ferries from Portsmouth or Plymouth and go to either Santander or Bilbao (both on the north-coast of Spain) A one-way trip takes about 24 hours and booking a cabin is recommended.

They also have dog kennels on-board but you CANNOT keep your dog in the ferry cabin with you.

The biggest consideration for the ferry (apart from the cost), is the weather. You will be crossing the notorious Bay of Biscay, and it can get ROUGH. Even in the middle of summer.

As someone who gets seasick *(hilarious considering I'm ex-Navy and have lived on boats for 15 years),* I avoid this crossing and prefer to drive from the UK through France to Spain, but it's entirely up to you.

Driving through France to Spain

If you decide that you want to drive your motorhome or camper down to Spain, you first need to decide if you're going to take the ferry or tunnel from UK to France.

Then you have two main routes through France to Spain. Each route takes about a day to drive:

Route 1 is via Tours, Bordeaux and down the Atlantic coast on the N10 until you cross the border between Biarritz and San Sebastien. You can join this route easily if you decide to come over on a ferry to Caen, Le Havre, Dieppe or Cherbourg.

Route 2 is straight south from Calais, skirting around Paris and then down to Clermont Ferrand and Perpignan on the A75 (which is largely free from tolls). The huge highlight from this route is crossing the Millau Viaduct-it's well worth the experience.
Of course, you can always drive down one route and back up another!

Can I drive to Spain in the Winter?
Yes. I know there are those pesky Pyrenees mountains in the way, but the main routes are all kept open, unless you happen to be really unlucky and arrive in the middle of a snowstorm (do check the weather forecast before you leave).
If this happens, then we recommend stopping for the night somewhere safe (again, the beauty of travelling in a motorhome) and then moving on when the snow has stopped and the roads have been cleared.

Don't forget about the new French law insisting you have either winter tyres fitted or carry snow chains / snow socks.

Driving tips for Spain

- Spain drives on the right.
- Seatbelts are compulsory.
- Driving in flip-flops or open-backed shoes is illegal.
- Speeds are in km/h, not mph (you might want to change the setting on your sat-nav).

- You need lights on in the tunnels (there are signs to remind you).
- You cannot touch a screen while driving (television, video, DVD etc.) This also includes a motorhome sat-nav- program it before you leave and don't touch it unless you're parked up safely.
- Road surfaces are generally pretty good and, unlike France, they try to avoid having 10,0000000 roadworks on a bank holiday weekend.
- On hills, use the crawler lanes to get out of the way of faster-moving traffic.
- Avoid cities if you're driving in a motorhome- many of them are too crowded and the streets are just not cut out for large vehicles. Park outside and use public transport to get in.
- Yellow diamond signs mean you have priority. Diamonds with a black line through mean you no longer have priority (this is usually on roundabouts).
- Trams always have priority everywhere- keep eyes in the back of your head if you're driving near a tram network.
- If you are driving in the mountains, you MUST sound your horn before a blind bend.
- You may carry a load, such as bikes on a rack, extending by up to 10% of the length of the vehicle to the rear. **The load must be indicated by a board / panel with diagonal red and white stripes.**

- The use of winter tyres in Spain is regional. Look out for traffic signs indicating that winter tyres or snow chains are compulsory where you are.

Red / white warning board signs for bike racks or anything overhanging the end of the motorhome or campervan is a legal requirement in Spain. Lines must point into the middle of the road.

Motorhomes or campers with a total train length of over 12m

If you're travelling in / through Spain and your outfit exceeds 12m, you need to have marker boards fitted to the back of your vehicle. You can either have two small boards or one large board but they must be placed at the back of the outfit between 50cm and 150cm off the ground.

Your marker board must be yellow in the centre with a red outline, be made out of aluminium and be manufactured to ECE70 standard.

Roads in Spain

The Spanish road network is pretty good and has a mixture of paid and free roads.

Autopistas ('Peaje' or 'AP') are toll roads, marked red on the map and they will have the letter 'P' next to the number.

Toll-free motorways are marked with the letter 'A' and are marked blue on the map. Main routes/dual carriageways are green on the map.

An "autovía" is like a motorway, except that bicycles and agricultural vehicles can use it.

Restricted driving days in Spain

Spain has certain days where driving is restricted. Please check in advance.

Restricted Zones in Spain

Some of the bigger cities in Spain have environmental zones which only residents are allowed to drive in. These zones are indicated with 'Area de prioridad residencial' and are banned to anyone without a permit (or special exemption).

Toll roads in Spain

If you choose to use the Autopista toll roads, here are some tips for you:

- The weight of your motorhome no longer matters- all motorhomes are charged the same.
- Just like other tolls in Europe, you'll usually get a ticket when you enter the toll route, then have to pay when you exit at either a manned or automatic toll booth. Occasionally, some sections of road have a fixed fee, so you pay when you enter.
- Tolls can be paid for in cash (Euros) or cards at selected booths. American Express is rarely accepted but UK credit or debit cards should work (but not always, so carry cash to be safe!)

Alternatively, get a toll pass / payment tag so you can use the 'Telepeaje', 'VIA-T' or 'T' lanes. We use e-Movis and it's well worth it- especially on busy days where you can drive right on by the queues.

Bizarrely, some toll roads in Spain are being 'demoted' to free routes but are still marked as AP on the map.

Speed Limits in Spain

Cars and vehicles under 3.5 tonnes:

- 120 km/h (74mph) on motorways/ autovias and many dual carriageways 100km/h (62mph) on major roads.
- 90 km/h (56 mph) on minor roads (out of town)
- 50 km/h (31 mph) in built-up areas
- 25km/h in signposted residential zones

Motorhomes and Campervans weighing over 3.5 tonnes:

- motorways 90 km/h (56 mph)
- major out-of-town roads 80 km/h (50 mph) minor out-of-town roads 70 km/h (43 mph) urban areas- 50 km/h (31 mph).
- 25km/h in signposted residential zones.

Motorhomes with trailers or caravans (over 750kg)

- motorways 80 km/h (50 mph)
- major out-of-town roads 80 km/h (50 mph)
- minor out-of-town roads 70 km/h (44 mph)
- built-up areas- 50 km/h (31 mph)

Speed Cameras in Spain

Yes, there are many, mainly fixed. Radar detectors are illegal.

GERMANY

Useful things to know

Emergency Numbers: 112 will get you everything.
Language: German. English is widely understood and spoken.
Currency: Euro
Cards: most major credit and debit cards are accepted. American Express is only taken in large stores (not often at fuel stations).
Time zone: GMT+1 (or one hour ahead in BST).
Tipping: If you decide to treat yourself to a meal out and the service has been good, tipping 10-15% is standard. Coffee shops and lunchtime eateries often don't include a tip, so check your bill before paying. Cash is best- the server rarely gets any tips added on by card.
Customs: There is no border between Germany and its EU neighbours. There are official border points on major roads into Switzerland, although we went the back roads and just drove right in!
Shops: Many shops, bars and restaurants close on Sundays, especially after lunchtime.
Laundry: SB waschsalon is what you need to search for in Google.
There are some localised laws in more rural areas- such as no vacuuming or washing on Sunday (day of rest) and no playing loud music during siesta time (12-3pm). Don't worry, the Germans will tell you if you are breaking any rules.

Germans can sometimes come across as abrupt, but it's a cultural thing- try not to take it personally. They are also EPIC at queuing and being on time; even better than the British. Public transport is almost always to the minute- so don't be late!

Don't stand too close in queues or when talking to people- they value personal space.

Using the Nazi salute, saying or shouting “heil Hitler” and wearing or displaying the swastika or other symbols of the Third Reich is a criminal offence, punishable by up to five years in prison. They do not take 'it was a joke' as an acceptable excuse.

The Germans do not shy away from their history, but they are keen not to make light of it. There are plenty of museums and historical reminders to the Holocaust, concentration camps and the wars, but they insist (rightly so) you treat these places with respect; no vandalism, sitting on them, and sometimes even taking 'selfies' is frowned upon.
Jaywalking (crossing the road without a pedestrian crossing) is illegal in Germany and you may be fined.
Drones: Drones and similar remote-controlled flying devices are allowed in Germany are long as you stay at least a minimum of 100m from people, vehicles and buildings that are not connected with the drone operator.

Flying must happen in daylight only and up to a maximum height of 100m. Never fly closer than 1.5km to airports.

The drone must always remain within the sight of the operator.
If you have a drone above 2kg, you must have a qualification. All drones above 250g must be clearly labelled.

Germany - why you should go!

Germany is one of my all-time favourite countries in Europe. The history is mind-boggling, the people are friendly and the castles. Oh my goodness, the castles are out of this world.
Plus, there's yummy food, roads without speed limits (I'll admit, more use on a motorbike rather than a motorhome), beer halls (which are terrific fun) AND there are toboggan runs- I'm officially addicted. Suffice it to say, we've been back to Germany several times and there's not been anywhere in the country I've not enjoyed.

Germans love their wohnmobils (motorhomes in German) and provide plenty of parking and overnight stopovers for them. There are around 1500 Stellplätzen around the country- and that's not including campsites or other approved stopovers.

Where to go

If you're driving from the UK to Germany (we'll cover that shortly), you need to allow at least a day to get from arriving in France (by either ferry or Eurotunnel) to the west German border. Of course, if you only have a week's holiday, that only allows a few days to explore the country, so we'd suggest staying to the west of the country.

If you have 10-14 days or longer to tour Germany, you can get a lot further east, certainly as far as Füssen and Neuschwanstein Castle on the Romantic Road and possibly even further if you're happy to drive every day. We have made it all the way to the Eagle's Nest on the SE corner and back in 2 weeks, but it was a lot of driving!

Highlights of a motorhome tour of Germany

Some of our favourite places that we've visited in Germany (so far!) include:

- The Black Forest. The entire area is incredible. Whether you drive it with a motorhome or a motorbike, the B500 is one of the BEST roads we've ever been on!
- Camping next to the Kiel Canal with our motorhome. The size of those ships...!
- Munich. There's something about this city that keeps us coming back. I think it's the beer halls...
- Hohenzollern Castle. Possibly my favourite castle in Germany.
- Any of the rodelbahns (the toboggan runs). They're so much fun.
- Cologne. The cathedral is incredible.
- Anywhere which sells bratwurst...

When to go to Germany

The weather and seasons in Germany are very similar to the UK, although with generally warmer summers. Summer is wonderful and if you don't want to visit any cities, it's a great time to explore (the cities get CRAZY crowded during summer).

Having said that, we visited Miniatur Wunderland in Hamburg and toured along the Kiel Canal in July and it was perfect weather and not too busy.

As always, we prefer to tour in Spring or Autumn. The weather is generally sunny and warm and the days are still long enough to make the most of them. The mountains may still have snow- we went up Zugspitze (the highest mountain in Germany) in April and it was still covered in snow.

In winter, expect snow, rain and cold, so make sure you pack appropriately, including fitting winter or all-season tyres. Despite the dreariness, we also love Germany in December, so we can visit the incredible Christmas markets (Germany has some of the best and biggest Christmas markets in Europe!)

Motorhome stopovers & overnight parking in Germany

There are several types of motorhome and campervan stopovers you can use:

- Campsites

- Stellplatz
- Autohof/ Free approved motorhome parking schemes.
- Motorhome Wild camping

Motorhome Campsites

Campsites in Germany are much like campsites anywhere else in Europe. We've always been amazed at the standard of the campsites; the ones we've stayed at have been very well-equipped with great facilities. They also seem to have lovely restaurants either on-site or very close by. Of course, some campsites will be more rustic and have more basic facilities- choose wisely!

Motorhome Aires in Germany- Stellplatz

Aires in Germany are called Stellplatz, but they work exactly the same way as motorhome aires in France.

Autohof

An alternative to Stellplatz are the Autohof, a private network of service stations. These places are situated near the Autobahn (they are NOT the Autobahn services, we don't recommend staying on those) and they're usually just a few minutes from an exit.

There is a fee for using an Autohof, but sometimes you can claim it back if you use the restaurant or shop on site. If you'd like to avoid campsites and stellplatz, but don't want to risk staying off-grid, there are two schemes which offer places to stay with a motorhome or campervan (and even a caravan!):

- **Landvergnügen** (Country fun) is a German motorhome stopover scheme which runs very similarly to Brit Stops in the UK or France Passion. It's a collection of businesses and locations across Germany which allow motorhomes and campervans to stay overnight on their land. In return, you are expected to eat a meal at the restaurant, or buy some wine or produce from their shop. If you enjoy visiting vineyards, farms, restaurants or local markets, this might be a good scheme for you.
- **Winzeratlas** is a very similar concept, but this one is entirely for wine lovers. All the places are winegrowers, winegrowers and taverns and they allow you to stay overnight after sampling their produce. To be fair, it's a wonderful way to enjoy the evening without having to drive back to a hotel!

Driving tips for Germany

German drivers are mostly pretty confident and drive accurately and fast. The roads are well maintained and roadworks are well-organised and planned.

- Germany drives on the right, so stay right and let them overtake on the left.
- Check your mirrors regularly; other drivers will usually indicate to show they are going to overtake.
- Do not undertake!

- All vehicles turning right must give priority to bikes (on their inside) going straight on.
- If you see hazard lights ahead, this means an accident or traffic jam. Slow right down and put on your hazard lights too, to alert the person behind you.
- A sign saying 'Umleitung' (or just 'U') means diversion. 'Geschlossen' means closed'.
- Ausfahrt' (yes, I giggle every time) means exit. You'll see this on every road exit. There will be a different speed limit for the slip road.
- Seatbelts are compulsory.
- In-car speed camera detectors and motorhome sat-nav systems warning of the presence of radars are illegal.
- Dash-cams are allowed but must not obscure the driver's vision and any footage used in videos must obscure faces and number plates.
- Using or holding a mobile phone while the engine is on is illegal.

Minor traffic offences can result in on-the-spot fines.

Toll Roads in Germany

You'll be pleased to know that, for vehicles under 7.5 tonnes, there are no tolls or vignettes to pay in Germany, except for a couple of tunnels. However, they have been talking about adding tolls onto their most popular Autobahns for years, so I expect some to pop up in the future.

Don't forget, both Austria and Switzerland require a vignette, so be sure to get one before/ as you cross the border.

Autobahns

Autobahns are motorways and many don't have speed limits. At all. You can go as fast as is safe. However, there are areas where speed limits are now enforced- you'll see the speed signs on the side of the road and these must be obeyed- there will be cameras.

LEGAL SPEED SIGNS: A round white sign with red border and black numbers (such as '130') means that is the legal speed limit and must be adhered to.
SUGGESTED TOP SPEED: square blue sign with white numbers reading '130' means that's the suggested top speed.
Also, be sure to leave extra braking room; they might not have speed limits but they take a very stern view on anyone causing an accident.

Speed limits in Germany

Speed Limits are as follows (unless otherwise signed!)

- Motorways/ autobahns- none unless indicated
- Major roads- 100 km/h (62 mph)
- Built up areas- 50 km/h (31 mph)

Speed cameras in Germany

Despite the lack of restriction on the Autobahns, there are PLENTY of speed cameras elsewhere.

Rest Stops

The autobahn has rest stops (Raststätten) with fuel stations, restaurants, shops, picnic tables and toilets (expect to pay an entrance fee!) There are also picnic areas along many roads, but these often have no facilities.

Drink driving laws

Germany has stricter drink driving laws than the UK, only allowing 0.5 milligrams of alcohol per millilitre of blood (the UK is 0.8). As always, don't drink and drive.

Low Emission Zones

Germany does have Umweltzonen (low emission zones) in some bigger cities. Sometimes, there's no warning until you're already in one! Luckily, they're policed by wardens rather than cameras.

You can buy an umweltplakette (sticker) to put on the windscreen to drive into these (currently it costs 6€ and takes about 2 weeks to arrive).

Rettungsgasse

German (and Austrian) law requires drivers to create a Rettungsgasse (emergency vehicle lane) whenever there is an accident or emergency on the Autobahn. This is so ambulances, police or fire can get to the casualties.

NOTE: This is only for when you are pulling to a stop or very very slow moving.

If there are two lanes (going in the same direction), drivers must move their vehicles to the far right or far left (whichever is closest to you), creating a middle open lane for emergency vehicles.

If there are more than two lanes then drivers in the right-side lanes stay far right, while drivers in the middle or left lane(s) go on the far left. The emergency parking lane (hard shoulder) should not be blocked unless signage or a police officer indicates otherwise.
You should keep all doors closed and avoid standing outside the vehicle so you don't get in the way of any emergency service vehicles.

Getting Fuel

There are plenty of fuel stations across Germany. As with everywhere, you'll find the prices slightly higher on the Autobahns, although we found even those to be cheaper than in France or the UK.

Benzin is Petrol (gasoline). It's often super (95) or Super plus (98) - Green handles on pump.
Diesel is called diesel. Black or yellow handles on pump.
Some places are 24h pay at the pump but may require you to go into the shop and pay the cashier either in advance or after you've filled up- there will be a sign to tell you what to do. (Leave your car in front of the pump and make a note of the pump number.)

You can pay using cash or a credit card. Many places do NOT take American Express. Non-autobahn stations in Germany may or may not accept card payment. You can usually use your UK cards without a problem.

Getting LPG in Germany

LPG (GPL) can be found at selected petrol stations and at autogas stations. If buying from a petrol station, you may need to wait for an attendant to turn the system on for you.

Germany uses the ACME LPG adaptor for self-refillable gas bottles.

German Black Forest Itinerary idea

If you've never been to Germany before, here's the 10-day itinerary we did in the Black Forest and the Romantic road (south Germany).

- Start off in the Black Forest. Our first stop was Todtnau, where we rode the Hasenhorn Rodelbahn toboggan run (which was awesome!). There's also a lovely walk at Todtnau waterfall.
- Visit Triberg- the home of the world's largest and smallest cuckoo clocks.
- Visit Hohenzollern Castle- the castle perched on the hill.
- Head off down the Romantic Road. There are too many highlights to count, including some of the best waterfalls in Europe, but you have to visit Neuschwanstein Castle- the one which inspired Walt Disney (be sure to go inside too- it's breathtaking).

We also tied this trip in with a visit to the Rhine Falls in Switzerland, a trip around Lake Constance, wild camping for the night in Austria and we ended with a trip up Zugspitze- the highest mountain in Germany.

Food and Drink in Germany

Bratwurst. That is all you need to know. It's spicy pork sausage with bread and maybe a sauce (my husband loves the Currywurst). There are apparently over 1500 different varieties! Bratwurst mit pommes (sausage and chips) is served EVERYWHERE- even many service station restaurants.

They also love kebabs. There are over 16,000 kebab restaurants in Germany- apparently, they sell 30 döner kebabs a second!!!
For unique foods, you have to try Black Forest Gateau in the Black Forest (Triberg is famous for it). Also, try sauerkraut (pickled cabbage). It's an... acquired taste but not as bad as it sounds- promise!

Germany is famous for its local beer and they take it very seriously. There are other options on the menu if you're a non-beer drinker (like me.) Don't ask for tap water, they consider that rude. Mineral water (still or sparkling) is always available by the bottle.

If you visit a beer festival and some the bigger beer halls, you will be charged a 'pfand' which is a deposit for the glass. Often, you keep one glass and they come around with huge jugs to refill your glass. They also love brandy and schnapps. You might also be charged a pfand at a

supermarket if you buy bottles- you can take them back for a refund if you wish.
Germany is great for eating out- and prices are very reasonable. We love the informality of the beer halls (mainly found in cities- Munich is our favourite so far), but I think only once have we had a 'bad' meal- Germans take their food seriously and bad places don't last long.

Parked up near Neuschwanstein Castle, Germany

NORWAY

Useful things to know

Emergency Numbers: 112 will get you everything
Language: Norwegian. English is widely understood and spoken flawlessly.
Currency: Norway uses the Norwegian Krone (NOK), NOT the Euro. Obviously, the exchange rate fluctuates, but as a (very) rough guide, 10 NOK is about £1.
Cards: most major credit and debit cards are accepted. American Express is only taken in large stores (not often at fuel stations).
Time zone: GMT+1 (or one hour ahead of the UK).
Tipping: Tipping is not customary but always appreciated. It's common to round the bill to the nearest 10NOK.

Touring Norway with a dog

Yes, you can take your dog into Norway. You will need to get a tapeworm tablet administered by a vet 1-5 days before arrival (just like when you return to the UK). And yes, you will need ANOTHER one to go into the UK after driving back through Europe.

Norway is pretty dog friendly. You must keep your dog on a lead when walking between 1 April and 20 August to protect wildlife. Apart from that, they are allowed almost everywhere, including on the beaches.

Drones - Drones and similar remote-controlled flying devices must be kept at least a minimum 150m from people, vehicles and buildings that are not connected with the drone operator. Flying must happen in daylight only and up to a maximum height of 120m. Never fly closer than 5km to airports. The drone must always remain within the sight of the operator.

Motorhoming in Norway

If you want to take your motorhome to some of the most breathtaking scenery in the world (not just Europe), you have to find time to go to Norway.

The fjords, the mountains, the glaciers- it's just all... I run out of superlatives. And even better, they LOVE motorhomes and campervans. Wild camping is allowed pretty much anywhere and there are so many incredible places to stay; choosing is often the hardest part.

Add in how friendly and welcoming the people are, and it's pretty much the perfect motorhoming destination.

Where to Go

If you're driving from the UK to Norway, you need to allow at least 3 days to get from arriving in France (by either ferry or Eurotunnel) to the Norwegian border. And that's 3 days of pretty much solid driving.

We don't recommend visiting Norway if you only have a week or even 10 days for your road trip. It's too far and all you'll do is drive there and back. Of course, if you're going to rent a motorhome and fly in, that's perfectly doable in a week.

If you have a couple of weeks, you can certainly explore some of the best places in southern Norway but, again, it will be a lot of driving. We went for 3 weeks, and we still didn't get as far as we wanted to.

Don't forget, the best views are on the coastal roads, but they are also the slowest roads. So ideally save your motorhome trip until you have a block of 3 or more weeks so you can really enjoy it.

Norway is the longest country in Europe, and it takes about 30 hours to drive from Kristiansand to Hammerfest in the north; if you go the direct roads down the middle (which is also the expensive toll road!) It took us 2 days to drive back from near Kristiansund to the Swedish border.

Don't overestimate how far you can travel in one day. The roads are much slower than you might be expecting, not helped by all the ferries between places. There are a lot of single-track roads which will slow you down.

TOP TIP: If you're trying to get to the north of Norway, go up through Sweden- the roads are faster and also toll-free.

Some of our Favourite Places in Norway

Here are some of the highlights from our time in Norway (so far!):

- Trollstigen Road- one of the craziest roads in Europe.
- Driving the longest road tunnel in the world
- Steinsdalsfossen Waterfall- the one you can walk behind.
- Sverd i fjell- the swords in the rock.
- Flamsbana Railway- voted one of the best train rides in the world.

The Visit Norway website is a wonderful resource for finding places to visit, plus motorhome services, petrol stations and other useful tips.

When to Visit

We have been to Norway several times- once with a motorhome, twice by air. We planned our motorhome trip in mid-July… and it rained solidly for 3 weeks (and yes, it was STILL one of the best trips we've done!)
We've also been in late November and early March, both times to see the Northern Lights (Norway is one of the best places in Europe to see the Northern Lights.)

So, the answer on when is the best time depends on what you want to do. Norway only really has two seasons-summer and winter. Spring and Autumn do happen, but they are quick and unpredictable.

Norway in Winter

Norway is further North than Scotland, so expect cold and snow in winter- a lot of it. Anytime after October until early April is considered winter.

Also, don't forget that Norway doesn't get much sunlight in winter, and what it does get is pretty weak. So you don't have as long during the 'day' to explore, even if you are happy to drive in the snow and ice. The main roads are kept pretty clear, but more remote areas might be impossible to access, even with winter tyres fitted on your van.

Visiting Norway in Summer

Summer is by far the best time for a road trip to Norway. The days are long, the weather is surprisingly warm and even though it rained a lot for us, it was still pleasant to explore. *(It doesn't ALWAYS rain in summer- I'm just a rain magnet!)* The roads are usually fully open from May until October.

Mid-summer is a HUGE deal in Norway (and most of Scandanavia). There are parties to celebrate the midnight sun (especially north of the Arctic Circle), but the long hours and light evenings can make it hard to sleep; make sure you find a way to get your rest if you're doing a lot of driving.

Don't worry about crowds if visiting in August or peak season; the cities might be busy (especially those with

cruise ship ports), but otherwise, the country is blissfully uncrowded and there are plenty of places to stay.
It is possible to see the Northern Lights as early as September, especially if you're in the far north of Norway.

Planning a Route

There is no direct ferry from the UK to Norway, so you'll need to drive via Denmark.
Once you're in Denmark, you have a couple of options- take the ferry from Hirtshals to Kristiansand or driving through Sweden, over the bridge.
Ferry to Norway from Denmark
The fastest route to Norway from the UK is using the Colorline Hirtshals- Kristiansand ferry. Hirtshals is a town right at the top of Denmark and driving to Hirtshals from Calais takes 12 and a half hours (1264km).

NOTE: Don't confuse Kristians**A**nd with Kristians**U**nd (both in southern Norway). I set the wrong course in our motorhome sat-nav and we went miles out of our way!

The Hirtshals ferry takes about 2 hours, which isn't too long in case the dreaded North Sea is having a bad day!
There is also a ferry from Hirtshals to Bergen, but it meant missing out on a lot of the stuff we wanted to see further south.

When we went in 2018, we paid 462.20€ (yes, Euros, not NOK), which was for 3 adults and an 8m motorhome PLUS a motorbike trailer. That was for one way.

In 2021, a 7m motorhome WITHOUT a trailer, with 2 adults, costs around 219.80€ one way.

Øresund toll bridge- driving via Sweden

If you don't want to take the ferry, the only other way to get into Norway with your vehicle is to drive via Sweden. This route is about 1580km from Calais to the Norwegian border and Google maps thinks it will take just under 18 hours (that's probably very optimistic!)

The upside to this route is you don't have to pay for a ferry. The downside is you have to pay for tolls on both the Øresund toll bridge and the smaller Storebælt toll bridge in Denmark.

When we went in 2018, the Øresund Bridge and the A/S Storebaelt cost us £275 one way.

Currently (2021), a 7m camper or motorhome (without trailer) costs 108€ (it can be cheaper if you pay in advance).

Storebælt toll bridge- 2021 prices for a motorhome between 6-10m (without trailer) and under 3.5tonnes is 85€.

Other routes into Norway

Of course, if you have a couple of months, you can get into Norway from another direction. Perhaps you choose to drive up through Sweden, then enter up at the North and drive south through Norway. Or you could even go via Poland, Latvia and Finland and make it a proper adventure!

Norway Border Control/ Customs

Norway is not in the EU and therefore there IS a hard border between it and its neighbouring countries (unlike much of Europe).
With this in mind, you are only allowed to carry a certain amount of alcohol and tobacco into the country, even if it's for personal use.

You also need to complete a customs declaration form before you enter the country (which we only discovered at the ferry port and had to hastily complete. One of the funniest things was watching people who didn't realise there was an alcohol allowance and had too much with them; they decided to make a party of it and were giving away their alcohol (and drinking as much of it as they could!) rather than pay the fine.

Norway Customs App

By far the easiest way to declare and pay any customs charges is via the Norwegian Customs app. You can download it onto your phone/ iPad, fill it in, pay anything owed and then you can use the green channel when you arrive in Norway.

Wild Camping in Norway

This is one of the best parts about motorhoming in Norway- the FREEDOM of camping and the right of access.
If you enjoy staying off-grid and wild camping with your motorhome, Norway is going to be your heaven. It has a

freedom to roam law, allemannsrett (all man's rights) meaning you can wild camp anywhere where the land is not owned, cultivated or where there is a sign forbidding it.

You still need to follow these rules:

- Stay at least 150m from dwellings.
- Stay no longer than 48 hours in one place.
- Don't stay if there is a sign stating no overnight parking.
- Don't put out awnings, chairs and so on, that's 'camping'.
- Be vigilant about campfires in summer.

Motorhome and Campervan Service Points in Norway

Norway is an incredibly clean country remarkably free from litter and we urge everyone visiting to help keep it that way. There are plenty of rubbish bins, dump stations and water taps almost everywhere. We found them using the Park4night app. Most rest areas had free toilets to use if you wish.

There was only one area where we needed water and couldn't find it, near Flam and the mean man at the campsite wouldn't let us pay to fill up our tank. But otherwise, it was very easy.

At some of the motorhome service areas (Tømme stations) you might need a key from the garage or attendant, especially if using the black waste.

I don't think we found any taps which WEREN'T drinking water; pretty much all the water in Norway is potable- and is provided freely, so there's no need to buy bottled water. **NOTE:** In winter, some water supplies may be turned off at times if the supply might freeze.
Most running water in the mountains and forests of Norway is clean enough to drink but avoid water running through pastures or runoff from glaciers, as this may contain harmful microorganisms.

Driving Tips for Norway

We enjoyed driving in Norway. The roads are much less congested than the rest of Europe, and there's so much space to spread out and explore. The tolls, tunnels and ferries take a little while to get used to, we'll go into those in more detail shortly.

Norwegian drivers are pretty calm and happy to wait or give way as necessary. Roads are generally well maintained and roadworks are few, but there are some very narrow roads, especially along the edges of the fjords.
You'll need to get used to how wide your motorhome is- and get used to other vans and lorries coming at you on very narrow roads.

Be aware of the weather conditions. The mountains can turn hostile very quickly in bad weather. Some mountain passes could close with no warning in inclement weather. Also, pay attention to your brakes, going up and down mountain passes can make them very hot. To avoid this, drive in a low gear, don't 'ride the brakes' and brake with less force to help the brakes stay cool.

When driving uphill, watch the vehicle's temperature gauge to avoid engine overheating. If you're planning to go up (or down!) Trollstigen (and you should!) choose your time wisely, early morning just at sunrise is the best time.

Also, don't overestimate how far you can travel in one day. The roads are much slower than you might be expecting- not helped by all the ferries between places. It takes around 30 driving hours to go from Oslo up to Lofoten, so plan accordingly.

Here's an overview for Norway driving rules:

- Norway drives on the right, so stay right and let them overtake on the left.
- You must drive with dipped headlights ALL THE TIME- even on sunny days.
- Speeds are in kms- you might want to adjust your motorhome sat-nav settings.
- Seatbelts and child safety seats are compulsory
- Using a mobile phone while the engine is on is illegal.
- UK driving licences are perfectly acceptable to use and you probably won't need an IDP (find out

the changes made to driving in Europe after BREXIT).

- In cities where there is more than one lane, you'll often find one reserved solely for buses and taxis- don't use this!
- Traffic joining from the right has priority on junctions with no 'give way' signs or painted lines across the junction..
- Passing places on single-tracked roads are marked by a white M on a blue background.
- There are not currently any restricted emissions zones in Norway, although central Oslo does close to diesel traffic when monitored emissions are considered high.
- Norway has a "human-oriented" culture which puts pedestrians and cyclists first. Pedestrians will expect you to slow down or stop so they can cross the street, and cyclists may not always follow traffic regulations!

Speed Cameras in Norway

Yep, they have them. Frequently. They are often on bridges, but police also do manual checks which can lead to on-the-spot-fines.

Drink Drive law in Norway

Alcohol laws are very strict in Norway, and penalties from driving under the influence are severe. The legal limit is 0.02% blood alcohol (the UK is 0.08%) and applies to the driver of any motorised vehicle. Medications to avoid if you intend to drive are marked with a red triangle.

Speed limits in Norway

The speed limits are low. Another reason you won't get anywhere as fast as you want to.

Speed Limits are as follows (unless otherwise signed!)

- Motorways/ major dual carriageways- 110km/h (70mph)
- Built up areas- 50 km/h (31 mph)
- Residential areas can be as low as 30 km/h

Speed limits for Vehicles over 3.5 tonnes and/ or towing

Heavy vehicles (over 3.5 tonnes) may not exceed 80 kilometres per hour regardless of the local limit- EXCEPT for motorhomes (camping cars) up to 7.5 tonnes, which are allowed to follow the same speed limits as other vehicles.

Vehicles towing caravans or trailers may not exceed 80 kilometres per hour regardless of the local limit. If the caravan or trailer is not equipped with brakes, the maximum speed is 60 kilometres per hour.

Tolls in Norway

If you're used to motorhoming in Germany (where there are very few tolls), Norway is going to be a shock.

There are about 200 toll stations in Norway. All of which are automated and marked with "AutoPASS" and the symbol to the right. Avoiding a toll often means driving hours out of your way AND taking 2 or even 3 extra ferries, so it defeats the point. On the plus side, motorhomes are charged the same price as cars and the total toll costs aren't usually that high.

The tolls all use number-plate recognition, so before you drive in Norway with a foreign vehicle, you should register with a toll pass. We used BroBizz.

How much are the tolls in Norway?

In total, we went through 23 tolls during our Norway road trip- and over half of those were on the E6, which is the main road running North-South through central Norway. The cost of that 2-day trip was £84.88 in toll charges.

The other tolls in Norway (around the western edge) came to a whopping £20.06- not bad for 12 days driving! But these are the roads with all the ferries on, so we also paid ferry costs on top of those toll charges.
So the total toll charges for our 2 week Norway road trip was £104.94.

How to pay tolls in Norway

There are two options to pay, either get a toll tag or be charged on the EuroPayment Collection (EPC) scheme. On the Atlantic Road, it may be possible to pay manually, but everywhere else charges your payment card online either as you use it or sends you a bill.

EPC Scheme (EuroPayment Collection)
Registration is optional but if you register for an EPC account this will normally reduce the time elapsed from the journey until you receive an invoice AND will make sure you pay the correct tariff; failure to register could result in you paying higher charges.

Autopass Toll tag
However, this scheme only lasts for 2 months. If you are planning to stay for longer than 2 months in Norway, they recommend getting a tag. Tags can often give discounts on the toll prices too and may be worth it for you.

When we visited, we had a motorhome over 3.5 tonnes, so got a toll tag with BroBizz. It worked well enough, but the charges were high; next time we go back we'll just use the EPC scheme as our new van is under 3.5 tonnes.

Ferries in Norway

Norway is a land of water. There are fjords and islands everywhere. If you've ever been motorhoming in Holland, you might not appreciate the problem... until you realise that these fjords are surrounded by mountains and it's not easy to build roads over them.
So they use ferries. It's no different from using a tunnel or toll road; it's just part of the road network in Norway.

The ferries in Norway are not like the ferries between the UK and France. You don't have to book in advance and they don't just go a couple of times a day. They're like shuttles, going back and forth continuously all day (although many do shut for a few hours late at night/ early morning.) You literally rock up, wait for the next sailing, then 'roll-on, roll-off'.

There are no 'cabins' or a requirement to book seats- you stay in your vehicle or can walk around the deck enjoying the view of the fjords. Some ferries take only 20 minutes, others can take nearly an hour.

How to use the ferries in Norway

They are really easy to use, even if they are expensive. You pull up and wait in the queue. If there's no ferry there, you're welcome to get out and walk around. Eventually, a ferry employee either will walk down the line, ask you your length and charge you the fee (one-way) or you pay when you are onboard. You can pay by card or cash (NOK).

CAUTION: Some places have ferries going to 2 or more destinations. Make sure you line up in the correct queue or you'll find yourself on a ferry in the wrong direction. Also, some ferries have a stop-off service, so they go to one place, and then another. Make sure you get off at the correct stop!

How much do the ferries in Norway cost?

The cost of the ferry depends entirely on the length of your outfit, as we discovered when we turned up in a 7.8m motorhome towing a 3m trailer. Ouch.

If you are under 6m, you'll pay the same price as a car, which is pretty reasonable. You can expect to pay around NKR100 for every ten minutes of ferry time in a sub-6m campervan or motorhome.
The cost advertised includes the driver, then you have to pay for additional passengers.

For us, we paid (as a 7.8m motorhome with a trailer):

- Ferry from Luavika to Oanes 358NOK
- Ferry from Puntnes (hjelmeland) – Nesvik on 13 – 430NOK
- Ferry Skanevik- Utaker (48) – 438NOK
- Ferry Arsnes- Gjermundshamn (DON'T PANIC- it goes to the island Varoldsoyna first!!) – 534NOK
- Ferry Fornes -Mannheller (route 5) – 384NOK
- Ferry Stranda – Liabygda – 412NOK
- Ferry E39 Vestnes- Molde – 602NOK
- Ferry E39 Halsa- Kanestraum – 438 NOK

TOTAL = 3596 NOK = £333.44

How to pay for the ferries in Norway

The ferries are not the same as tolls. You need to pay as you go, using a card or cash. We used our UK bank cards (Visa debit) without issue. They prefer cards as they don't always have change for cash.

Tunnels in Norway

Did I mention Norway is full of mountains and fjords? Often, instead of going over or round, they built the roads

THROUGH, so expect to spend more time than you might expect in tunnels.

You'll find some tunnels have roundabouts, slip roads, extreme inclines or declines and even rest stops inside; in the Laerdal Tunnel (the longest road tunnel in the world at over 15 miles long), those rest stops are blue!

If you don't want to go through the tunnel, you can take the Aurlandsfjellet Tourist Route which runs over the mountain above it.

Petrol/ Diesel in Norway

Fuel prices in Norway are relatively high due to environmental politics. Fuel stations are fewer in the mountains and other remote areas, especially in Northern Norway. Fuel gets more expensive the further north you go.

Unleaded is called Blyfri It's often super (95) or Super plus (98) - Green handles on pump.

Diesel is Diesel- Black or yellow handles on pump.

Some places are 24h pay at the pump but may require you to go into the shop and pay the cashier either in advance or after you've filled up, there will be a sign to tell you what to do.

You can pay using cash or a credit card. Many places do NOT take American Express. You can usually use your UK cards without a problem.

LPG in Norway

There are more than one hundred LPG stations across the country. Some are manned, some are automated and self-service. Some close at night or on Sundays, others are 24 hours. You can find them using the website **LPGnorge.no**

Some used the UK bayonet connector, others the Dutch bayonet. Many stations provide an "adapter" that will work regardless of your motorhome's system. You can bring your own adapter if you want to.
If using the MyLPG.eu website, check when the stations were last confirmed as being open (many are no longer there).

Note: There is NO LPG in Finland, so if you're planning your motorhome trip to include that country, top-up before you enter.

How Expensive is it?

Norway is consistently rated as one of the top 3 most expensive countries in the world. Norwegians are well-paid and pay high taxes, but the general cost of living is crazy high.

However, the tolls, ferries, fuel and vehicle costs are offset by the lack of campsite costs (if you're wild camping), but the biggest expense, apart from getting there, is likely to be food and drink.

Food and Drink in Norway

Food and alcohol are one of the most expensive things on any trip to Norway. One huge tip is to stock up in advance in Germany, Denmark or even Sweden. Remember the rules for taking alcohol across the border. This is one of the biggest advantages to touring Norway with a motorhome or campervan- you can save a lot of money by taking and preparing your own food.

Norwegians love their food and have many local specialities. Seafood is always good, but you could find reindeer (reinsdyrstek), torsketunger (cod's tongues), rakfisk (fermented trout) or a huge number of dried and cured meats and fish. Brown goats cheese (Brunost) is very common at meals.

Supermarkets / shops in Norway

For the best prices in Norway, try and shop in the Spar or Co-op's. There is no Lidl or Aldi in Norway (apparently, Lidl tried... and then gave up!)

Expect to pay at least double the amount you are used to in the UK for everything in a supermarket- even the local produce. Many stores have an 'own brand' which is slightly more reasonable- think Waitrose or M & S prices.

Most supermarkets and grocery shops do not open on Sundays. Garages will sell basic groceries (and hot dogs!) but at very inflated prices!

All drinks (cans and plastic bottles) have a deposit (pant) on them- in addition to the price on the label. You can put them back into the machine inside the supermarkets and get the option of a voucher to spend or giving the money to charity.

Alcohol in Norway

Tax is charged on all alcohol with more than 0.7% volume of alcohol, making all alcohol expensive.
Beer can be found in most supermarkets but is only sold before 8pm on weekdays or 6pm on Saturdays. For wine, spirits or strong beer, you must visit one of the Vinmonopolet outlets, found in most large cities and towns. To buy wine or beer in Norway, the minimum age is 18 years. For spirits, it is 20 years.

In a Vinmonopolet you will pay around NKR150 for a bottle of wine and NKR50 for beer and cider. Spirits cost considerably more.

Eating Out in Norway

I'll be honest, the only eating out we did was pizza- and it was so good we had it twice! The prices of restaurant and takeaway meals are crazy; even a McDonalds can cost upwards of £10 for a meal.
Burger and chips can be £25 per meal and a beer, cider or glass of wine in a restaurant will cost between NKR60-90.

ITALY

Useful things to know

Emergency Numbers: 112 will get you everything
Police 113, Fire Brigade 115, Ambulance 118
Language: Italian. English is usually spoken in campsites and in tourist areas, but not often elsewhere.
Currency: Euro
Cards: most major credit and debit cards are accepted. American Express is only taken in large stores (not at tolls and often not at fuel stations).
Time zone: GMT+1 (or always one hour ahead in BST).
Tipping: Service is usually included in a restaurant but do check. It's common to tip other services, like taxi drivers.
Shops: Food prices are pretty inexpensive. Many shops close on Sundays. Many shops and businesses also shut for a long lunch (between 12-2pm) and some will not open on Wednesday afternoons.

Touring Italy with a dog

Italy is pretty dog-friendly and they are widely accepted on public transport. Take a muzzle and their paperwork- although we've never been asked to show this. We also found dogs were allowed on the beaches except in high season and they're often allowed in restaurants if they're well-behaved and on a short lead.

Where to Go

If you're driving from the UK to Italy, you need to allow at least a day to get from arriving in France down to the north of Italy.

Of course, if you only have a week's holiday, that only allows a few days to explore the country, so we'd suggest staying to the north of the country. If you have 10-14 days or longer to tour Italy, you can get a lot further south, certainly as far as Naples/ Pompeii and possibly even further if you're happy to drive every day.

The more you tour around Italy, the more you'll realise there are some big differences between the North and South. There's much more wealth in the north. There are also more mountains and more big cosmopolitan cities.
Southern Italy is much less developed, with some incredible beaches and several islands for you to explore (or camp up next too if you can!)

When to Go

On our very first motorhome trip to Italy, we headed straight for the Italian lakes (one of the most popular areas in Italy) in August. Funnily enough, there were people EVERYWHERE. It was so crowded that we could barely find a Sosta with any room and all the campsites near the lakes had been fully-booked for months.
That was our fault- we hadn't planned ahead.

On the flip side, when we did our tour from Rome to Florence (via Pisa), we went in February. There was snow on the ground, it was freezing cold, but the lack of people when visiting the attractions made up for the chill factor. We practically had some of the museums and popular sites to ourselves!

For us, our favourite time to explore Italy is either later Spring or early Autumn. We toured the Dolomites in early October and the weather was perfect.

Obviously, the further south you go the warmer it will be. Sicily is where the Italians go to escape the chilly temperatures in the north. Of course, if you want to go skiing with your motorhome, stay in the Dolomites and enjoy some of the best slopes in Europe.

Sostas / Aires in Italy

Sostas are what the Italians call Aires. Many of them have services, although you'll find the quality varies dramatically, especially from north to south.

Below Rome, sostas and service points are much rarer, although free camping is also easier in many places. Camperonline.it is a good place to look if Park4Night isn't being helpful.

Normally, there is a one or two day stop restriction; aires are designed for you to see an area, and then move on- not stay for a week in one place.
We don't recommend you use the aires on the motorways as they are notorious for being unsafe.

Wild Camping in Italy

Wild camping in Italy is technically prohibited, although each region in Italy has their own regulations. It may be possible to get permission from the local governor if you ask at the town hall.

However, with a little common sense and discretion, it's often possible to stay off-grid with your motorhome or campervan.

- Don't try and wild camp on the coast unless you're somewhere REALLY remote (more likely to be allowed in the South). Having said that, wild camping in the National Parks (like the Dolomites) is strictly controlled.
- Don't try and wild camp in busy/ popular areas (like the Italian Lakes) unless you're visiting in the lowest of low season.
- Get the permission of the landowner if possible
- Don't stay within 1km of a built-up area, or within 100m of historic buildings.
- Don't park within 50m of national routes or within 150m of where drinking water is extracted.

We've heard of some people who have been approached and asked to pay a protection fee, to ensure their motorhome/ camper is 'left alone and undisturbed' whilst wild camping.

This seems to happen mostly when touring in southern Italy and in Sicily (mob country). I strongly suggest you pay this or move on; saying no is never going to end well!

Other Approved Overnight Motorhome Parking Schemes in Italy

If you'd like to avoid campsites and sostas, but don't want to risk staying off-grid, there are two schemes which offer places to stay with a motorhome or campervan.
The first is AgriCamper Italia, which has wonderful hosts all over the country, including farms, vineyards and artisans. Membership costs 29€ for the year (2021).

The second option is In Camper con Gusto, which does the same thing but focuses on the provinces of Piacenza, Parma and Reggio Emilia. Membership costs 35€/ year (2021).

Motorhome and campervan service points in Italy
If you're used to touring in France and Germany, you might be surprised at the poor state of some of the motorhome service stations in Italy, especially in the south of the country.

Often, there is either no black waste emptying point or it's blocked and out of service. The drains are in ridiculous places where it's impossible to get over- having a bucket or pipe is useful.

Driving tips for Italy

- Italy drives on the right, like much of Europe.
- Motorways are GREEN, dual carriageways are blue (opposite to the UK and much of Europe).

- The maximum speed for private vehicles under 3.5t is 130kph (81mph) on motorways but speed limits are lower for cars towing caravans and for motorhomes over 3.5t in weight.
- When on two-lane motorways, dipped headlights must be used.
- If driving through towns and villages, only use the horn in an emergency.
- Buses and trams have right of way.
- Seatbelts are compulsory.
- In-car speed camera detectors and motorhome sat-nav systems warning of the presence of radars are illegal.
- Using a mobile phone while driving is illegal, but you can use a hands-free unit.
- Minor traffic offences can result in on-the-spot fines.
- UK driving licences are perfectly acceptable to use.

Tolls in Italy

Italy doesn't have a vignette, it has tolls (pedaggio). You collect a ticket at the machine as you enter the road system and pay (either a person or machine) at the end in cash or on a card. Tolls are generally more expensive than Spain but cheaper than in France.

You can use a tollpass / telepass (like e-Movis) or you can pay-as-you-go by cash or card (we always recommend carrying some cash, just in case!) Signs indicate the means of payment accepted on each lane. Most motorhomes are calculated for class B, regardless of the number of axles.

Speed Limits in Italy

Speed Limits are as follows (unless otherwise signed!)

- 130 km/h (81 mph) on motorways
- 110km/hr (69mph) on major roads
- 90 km/h (56 mph) on minor roads (out of town)
- 50 km/h (31 mph) in built-up areas

In rain or snow conditions, the limit is lowered to 110 k/h on motorways and 90 k/h on trunk roads- this WILL NOT be signposted, you're expected to know it.

Motorhomes with trailers or caravans:

- motorways 80 km/h (50 mph)
- major out-of-town roads 70 km/h (44 mph)
- minor out-of-town roads 70 km/h (44 mph)
- built-up areas- 50 km/h (31 mph)

Motorhomes and Campervans weighing over 3.5 tonnes and under 12 tonnes:

- motorways 100 km/h (62 mph)
- major out-of-town roads 80 km/h (50 mph)
- minor out-of-town roads 80 km/h (50 mph)
- urban areas- 50 km/h (31 mph)

Driving in Italy

The Italians are known for being... exuberant with their driving. I will just say that we have been very grateful for our motorhome wing-mirror protectors every time we visit!

The scariest thing about the Italian driving style is that they generally seem to overtake on a blind bend and just hope that nothing is coming the other way. Our advice is to take it slowly, expect the unexpected, and be prepared to slam on the brakes at any moment.

We routinely just let people overtake, especially if we're towing a trailer with our motorhome, it's easier than worrying about which blind corner they'll try to kill themselves on next!

They seem to have very little concept of how long it takes for a large vehicle like a motorhome to slow to a stop, so try to leave a lot of braking room.

Horns

Italians love their horns. They'll beep to say hi to each other, they'll beep to tell each other off, they'll beep to let you know they're barrelling around a blind corner on your side of the road...! They also like to flash their headlights at you when they're on YOUR side of the road- as if you hadn't seen them.

Parking in towns and cities

Parking in most built-up areas is tough for vans. You'll see cars, buses and lorries parked in the most ridiculous

places, often blocking the road entirely whilst they unload or conduct their business.
If you are parking, white lines seem to denote free parking places, blue lines mean you need to pay (usually at a meter nearby).

I strongly recommend you don't take your motorhome into a city, but even in a town you might struggle finding somewhere to park. We often found an aire or campsite near a train line and used that to visit- like we did at Cinque Terre.

Road Conditions

Most roads in the north of Italy are of decent quality- similar to France or the UK. There is a noticeable difference between the roads in the north and south- they get steadily worse as you go down.
There are usually roadworks on the major motorways and often crash barriers and safety features are missing, so drive carefully.

Fuel Stations in Italy

Buy fuel anywhere apart from on the main roads, it'll be cheaper. Fuel prices are comparable to France. and slightly cheaper than the UK.

Secondly, there is a 'two-tier' payment system in Italy. A cheaper option if you fill yourself, and a more expensive rate if you get a forecourt attendant to do it for you.

BE CAREFUL WHERE YOU PULL UP, they get very upset if you park at an attended service fuel pump and then don't want it. There's often a symbol of a man with a pump, but 'con servicio' or servizio for service and 'self' for self-service.

Many stations close overnight and on Sundays. Chiuso means closed in Italian and Aperto means open.

Low Emission Zones and ZTLs in Italy

Many major cities and towns are trying to reduce pollution levels by restricting vehicles into the centre. This is a 'Zone Traffico Limitato' or ZTL. Most ZTLs are for residents only, so if you drive your motorhome into a ZTL you will receive a fine through the post. Also, NO rented vehicles are allowed in a ZTL at any time.

Low Emission Zones are becoming more common throughout Europe. If you do decide to drive your camper or motorhome into a city with no ZTL, check if there is an LEZ or congestion charge to pay. Alternatively, park outside the city and use public transport to access the centre.

Getting LPG in Italy

LPG (GPL) can be found at selected petrol stations and autogas stations. If buying from a petrol station, you may need to wait for an attendant to turn the system on for you.

Some people have apparently had trouble filling their refillable motorhome gas bottles. This is down to alternate tax rates for gas used for domestic heating and cooking, and the garages are concerned about the paperwork.

Apparently, things are worse if you have an interior fill point, which we do, but we've not had any troubles.

SWITZERLAND

Useful things to know

Emergency Numbers: 112 will get you everything
Phone code: +41
Capital: Bern
Language: The 4 official languages are French, German, Italian and Romansh. Different regions have different 'main' languages. English is widely spoken and understood.
Currency: Swiss Francs (CHF)
Cards: most major credit and debit cards are accepted. American Express is only taken in large stores (not often at fuel stations).
Time zone: GMT+1 (or one hour ahead in BST).
Tipping: Tipping is not expected but appreciated. 5% – 10% in restaurants is standard if you are happy with the service.
Shops: Food prices are pretty expensive (but not as bad as Norway.) Many shops close at 6.30pm and do not open on Sundays at all. Bigger supermarkets and garages may be open.

Drones: You are allowed to take and fly your drone in Switzerland, but they are VERY hot on privacy laws and recording people without their permission- especially if you then upload the footage to Youtube or something.
Drones and similar remote-controlled flying devices must be kept at least a minimum 100m from people, vehicles

and buildings that are not connected with the drone operator. Flying must happen in daylight only, below 150m and never fly closer than 5km to airports. The drone must always remain within the sight of the operator.

Where to Go

If you're driving from the UK to Switzerland, you need to allow at least a day to get from arriving in France to the Swiss border. And that's a long day of driving. It's about 7.5 hours (685km) from Calais to Basel, on the north-west border of Switzerland with France.

You can easily visit and explore Switzerland for just a few days or a week and it's quite easy to drive around. Of course, if you have 10-14 days, you can see a lot more of the country.

How long does it take to drive across Switzerland?
Switzerland isn't a huge country and you can drive across it quite quickly if you use the main roads.
As a guide, if you wanted to drive from Basel to Como (on the Italian border near Milan), it will take about 4 hours (300km).
If you want to drive across Switzerland from West to East, Geneva (on the western border with France) to St Moritz (in the East) will take about 5 and a half hours (480km).
However, much of the country is made up of the Alps (BIG mountains), so driving those take a lot longer as the roads are full of hairpin bends and steep inclines! Don't underestimate how long a journey will take you,

especially if you're in a larger vehicle like a motorhome or campervan.

TOP TIP: If you want to drive into northern Italy and the Dolomites, you might find it faster to go through France and then through Italy, rather than negotiating the Swiss Mountains.

Highlights of a Swiss road trip

Some of our favourite places to visit in Switzerland include:

- Standing in the middle of the Rhine Falls - one of Europe's biggest waterfalls.
- Driving in the Swiss Alps. They are breath-taking.
- Going up the Gelmerbahn Funicular and visiting Gelmersee Lake.
- Visiting Jungfrau and the train to the Glacier.
- Titlis - with the world's first cable car.
- Beautiful Chillon Castle - right on the shores of Lake Geneva.

Best time to visit Switzerland

Switzerland is worth visiting at any time of the year, but for different reasons. If you want to be able to drive freely and have all attractions open, go between April and October. Summer is very busy in the cities and major attractions, but the mountains are fairly empty.

Spring in Switzerland

Spring is lovely, as long as it's after April. Although technically Spring starts on 21 February, the snows don't fade until around the end of March, so April, May and June are a great time to visit. Avoid the Easter holidays if you can- prices get hiked up then.

But the flowers are beautiful, be sure to check out the Morges Tulip Festival at Lake Geneva in April. You can also visit Gruyeres on the first Sunday of May for the annual Cheese Festival- expect to try lots of yummy samples.

Summer in Switzerland
Summer highs hit mid-20s, although it can always feel cool up in the mountains. The skies are often clear and you can see the Milky Way at night. Of course, this means more people and more traffic, so if you are driving any of the crazy mountain passes, be sure to do it as early as possible to avoid oncoming tour buses!
A great day to be in Switzerland is Swiss National Day on 01 August. The entire country will celebrate with fireworks and parties - and they're happy for tourists to join in.

Autumn in Switzerland
Autumn is actually my favourite time in Switzerland. The days are still long and mostly warm, the leaves look amazing as they change colours, and the crowds from summer have gone.

The weather can be chilly going into November and many places close at the end of October, so do your research if there's something specific you want to do or see. If you enjoy wine, don't miss the Basel Wine Fair which happens at the end of October each year.

Winter in Switzerland

I'll be honest, winter in Switzerland starts around the end of November and runs until April. It gets COLD, there will be lots of snow and you'll need to prepare your van and yourself with appropriate gear. The days are also shorter, so you'll have less time to explore.

Some of the panoramic mountain trains, like the Gotthard Panorama and the Glacier Express shut over the winter months and many mountain roads are closed due to heavy snow. Many of the funicular railways and even some cable cars close during the winter too, due to adverse weather.

However, if you want to go motorhome or camper skiing, this is a great time to bring your van to the slopes! The best snow is usually from the end of December until March, but nature does love to be unpredictable! Skiing and winter sports are a BIG DEAL in Switzerland, so expect aires to be busy and campsites to be booked up well in advance. Also, try to visit during some of the world cup ski races- the atmosphere is amazing!

Don't miss out on visiting some of the Christmas markets. Switzerland has some of the best Christmas markets in Europe. It's also a great place to celebrate New Year, as some of the cantons in Switzerland celebrate it twice- once on 31st Dec/ 01 Jan, and then again on 13th Jan in

accordance with the Gregorian Calendar! (This is called Silvesterchlausen)
You must have winter / all season tyres fitted and / or carry snow chains.

Planning a Route to Switzerland

The quickest route from Calais to Basel (closest major point in Switzerland) is to the NE of Paris, via the A26 and then the N4. This route is around 685km, should take around 7h 25m and will cost about 33€ in tolls for a small camper or a car. A motorhome will cost more.
Route 2 is via A26, then N5 and is 725km long. This will cost a car or small camper around 48€ and is estimated to take 7h 39m.
Route 3 is via Belgium on the E411 and then the A4. It's longer, at 736km, will take 7h 42 but will only cost 9€ on the tolls. It's up to you which you choose.

Some top tips for route planning:

- Avoid peak days and times on the Eurotunnel.
- Try to avoid driving on the weekends or on bank holidays- LOTS of traffic.
- Alternatively, get up early and do as much driving as possible before the traffic hits, then stop and have a nap somewhere safe- a huge advantage of having a motorhome or campervan with a bed with you!!

Can I drive to Switzerland in the Winter?

Yes. Generally, the major routes are open all year, unless you happen to be really unlucky and hit it in the middle of a snowstorm (do check the weather forecast before travelling).

If this happens, then we recommend stopping for the night somewhere safe and continuing on when the roads have been cleared. Don't forget you will need snow chains and make sure you have fitted proper tyres.

Borders / Customs in Switzerland

Ok, let's get the technical bit out of the way.
Switzerland is in Europe, but it is NOT in the EU. Therefore, there are border restrictions on what you can / cannot take into the country (and out.)
It also does NOT use the Euro, it uses Swiss Francs. (CHF).

However, Switzerland IS in the Schengen Area, which means that if you are subject to a 90-day limit on your time in the Schengen Area (like UK passport holders are now after BREXIT), then your time in Switzerland DOES count towards those 90 days.

Tobaccos and spirit limits

If you are entering Switzerland, this is what you can carry with you (for persons older than 17 years):

- 250 units/g cigarettes / cigars / other tobacco products.
- 5 litres of alcohol (up to 18% vol.) and 1 litre of alcohol (over 18% vol).

Please check before you travel in case the rules have changed.

Border Crossings into Switzerland by Road

There are many places where you can drive across the border into Switzerland. Some have a proper, official border where you will be stopped and asked to show your passport and other documentation. Other crossings are literally marked with a flag which you look at as you drive past. There are no guards, no customs control and no barriers.

Don't forget you will need a vignette if you're planning to use the major roads, so you'll need to stop at a garage near the border to get one.

Bringing a dog / pet into Switzerland

You can bring your dog into Switzerland. They will need:

- Microchip
- Proof of rabies vaccination (now done as an Animal Health Certificate if you live in the UK).

Switzerland is pretty dog friendly. In restaurants, bars and cafes, you can usually assume your dog is welcome unless there's a sign (or employee) telling you otherwise. They are not allowed into public places like museums. Dogs are welcome on trains and most public transport. Inside a dog carrier, they're free of charge. On a leash will cost you a half-fare.

Vignettes in Switzerland

Switzerland uses a vignette system instead of tolls.
A vignette is literally a sticker which you must buy from an approved location and stick on your windscreen (in a

specific place so the cameras can see it, it's on the instructions when you buy).

Once it's in place, you can then drive on any of the motorways or major roads (Classes 1 and 2) without worry- there are no tolls to pay.

Some people make the process of getting a Swiss vignette sound horrendously difficult. It's really not, especially if your motorhome or campervan is under 3.5 tonnes. You can even order it online in advance and get it sent to your home before you leave.

How much does a Swiss Vignette cost?

A vignette currently costs 38.50€ per vehicle (2021). However, if you are towing a caravan OR a trailer (and the total train weight is less than 3.5t), you will need to purchase a second vignette. Also if, like us, you tow a motorbike or a second vehicle, you will need to buy another vignette for that too IF you plan to use it on the road on its own.

So we, with a motorhome, a trailer and TWO motorbikes, would have needed to buy 4 vignettes if we wanted to ride the bikes in Switzerland.

Affixing the vignette to a trailer or bike isn't as easy as on a car, it must be fixed "on an easily accessible part which cannot be dismantled and replaced."

How long is a vignette in Switzerland valid for?

A vignette is valid up until the end of January the year after you bought it. (So the 2021 sticker is valid until 31 January 2022.)

And yes, you still need to buy one even if you're only visiting Switzerland for one day, or even one hour, out of the year, assuming you want to use the motorways.

NOTE: the Vignette is invalid if you remove it. So be sure you won't be returning within the time limit before you take it off.

Do you HAVE to have a vignette in Switzerland?

If you want to use the motorway network, yes, it's compulsory. However, you can choose to drive just on the backroads and never buy a vignette- as long as your vehicle/ train weight is less than 3.5t.

What does a vignette NOT cover you for?

You will still need to pay for using any car trains, some of the bigger tunnels and any car ferries. There are also a few private roads which you will need to pay for if you choose to use them, like the Oberaar panorama road at the Grimsel pass.

Vignettes for vehicles UNDER 3.5 tonnes

If you have a vehicle with a train weight of less than 3.5t, and you haven't bought a vignette in advance, you can buy one from the border or just stop at the first garage / service station after crossing the border. Simples.

Vignettes for vehicles OVER 3.5 tonnes - Via App

If you have a motorhome which weighs over 3.5t, OR the total weight of your motorhome and trailer exceeds 3.5t, you can't buy the 'normal' vignette. You must pay the HVF (Heavy Vehicle Fee).

To do this, you need to download the VIA app (from your App store or Android store). This App is actually REALLY good. It allows you to select your vehicle type, enter details, select dates and pay, all from within the app. You get a scannable QR code for border crossings if needed to show proof of payment.

NOTE: If you are over 3.5t, you need to pay to use any public roads in Switzerland, not just the motorways.
I believe the current payment amount is CHF 3.25 a day (about £2.60) and there's a minimum fee of CHF 25.00.

Stopover Schemes

Swiss Terrior is the Swiss equivalent of France Passion. It's a scheme which connects vineyards, restaurants, farms and the occasional chocolate maker with motorhomers looking for safe places to stay overnight. If you'd like to avoid busy campsites and aires, but don't want to risk wild camping (which is illegal in Switzerland), this might be the option for you.

The scheme is simple. You join up and get access to a collection of businesses who have agreed to provide overnight parking for motorhomes and campervans at their premises, in return for you spending money with them.

The one downside to the scheme (according to people who've used it more extensively than we have) is that most of the places are in the west of Switzerland and there are very few businesses who've opted in around the major tourist areas- the ones where the campsites are often fully booked (like Jungfrau).

Wild Camping in Switzerland

This is a grey area. Usually, you can pull into a truck rest stop or parking area for a night without issue, but wild camping in cities or remote areas is banned.
However, many people wild camp up in the Alps, as we did, without issue.

National Parks and Game reserves
Overnight parking is prohibited in Swiss National Parks, Federal Game and nature Reserves and Wildlife protection or rest zones.
Also, it is forbidden to light a fire in these areas, unless in an official fireplace. Fines can be up to 10,000€.

Driving Tips for Switzerland

Switzerland has a good road network. Pay attention to your speed- fines are expensive! Driving just 11 km/h over the limit in a town could cost you CHF 250 as an on-the-spot fine

Some basic rules for driving in Switzerland:

- Switzerland drives on the right, like much of Europe.
- Overtake on the left (NEVER undertake).
- Seat belts are obligatory for all passengers. Children under 12 years old / under 150cm need an approved safety seat.
- You need to have a motorway vignette properly fitted on your vehicle, unless you are over 3.5t and have paid using the Via App.
- Headlights must be switched on during the day.
- Traffic from the right (including cyclists) has priority.
- Traffic on roundabouts has priority unless the signs indicate otherwise.
- Police cars, ambulances, fire trucks and trams always have priority.
- You're legally required to stop for pedestrians at a zebra crossing. NOTE: Trams do NOT have to stop, so don't walk in front of one thinking it must give way to you- it won't!
- Hands-free calling is allowed, but it is strongly discouraged. Handheld calling will attract a hefty fine.
- In some places, it is mandatory to turn off your engine when waiting for traffic lights, railroad crossings etc.
- In-car speed camera detectors and motorhome sat-nav systems warning of the presence of radars are illegal (whether they're in use or not!)

- Dash-cams are discouraged, as they impact people's privacy and there must be a clear legal reason for using them.
- Minor traffic offences can result in on-the-spot fines.

Speed Limits in Switzerland

Speed Limits for vehicles under 3.5t are as follows (unless otherwise signed!)

- Motorways/ autobahns- 120km/h (74mph)
- Major roads/ expressways- 100 km/h (62 mph)
- Outside built-up areas 80km/h (50mph)
- Built up areas- 50 km/h (31 mph)

Speed limits for vehicle OVER 3.5t

- Motorways/ autobahns- 100 km/h (62 mph)
- Major roads/ expressways- 100 km/h (62 mph)
- Outside built-up areas 80km/h (50mph)
- Built up areas- 50 km/h (31 mph)

Speed cameras in Switzerland

There are an estimated 1,000 speed cameras in Switzerland, which is a huge number for a small country. Again, pay attention to your speed.

Drink driving laws

Switzerland has stricter drink driving laws than the UK, only allowing 0.25 milligrams of alcohol per millilitre of blood (the UK is 0.8). As always, don't drink and drive. If you are a new or a professional driver, there is zero-tolerance, so be careful what medication you take.

Tips for Driving in the Mountains

Driving in the mountains can be scary- especially in a campervan or motorhome. Here are some tips to help.

- Estimated driving times by navigation systems and route planners can be very optimistic. Take your time and allow extra.
- On small roads, ascending traffic usually has priority. So if you are driving downhill, be prepared to give way to vehicles coming up towards you. The exception to this is the postbus, which has priority either way.
- Try not to drive in the mountains after dusk- it's even scarier at night!
- Many mountain passes close for winter. There are no fixed dates as it depends on snowfall Some higher passes can be closed until June.
- Some passes are too narrow or steep for trailers, caravans or motorhomes. Read any warning signs carefully.
- Make sure your vehicle is prepared and you have done your pre-trip checks.
- Make sure that you have adequate fuel- there are no fuel stations on mountain roads. Top up whenever you find a garage, even if it's only half empty.

Tips for braking / engine speed in the mountains

- When descending, use a low gear and high engine speed. The engine with help with deceleration, which in turns saves your brakes.
- Maintain as low a speed as possible. You will have longer braking time than you might be used to- allow extra room.
- Assuming a 5-gear vehicle, it is usually sufficient to use gear 1 to 3 only.
- Your brakes will get HOT as you descend as you are using them almost-constantly.
- Try not to 'ride' the brake and give them a rest whenever possible. If possible, stop about halfway down in a safe place for 10-15 minutes and let them cool.
- Keep a high engine speed and don't change gears so quickly (stay around 3000 - 4000 revs)
- If you gain speed, select a lower gear or gently use the brakes (not continuously).
- Do not drive in neutral.
- If you have an automatic motorhome or camper, switch to manual mode for better control over the gears.
- Hairpin bends are tough, especially if you don't have someone who can look for oncoming traffic. If in doubt, sound your horn before a blind bend and listen for a response.
- Don't underestimate the stupidity of other drivers, especially those who don't understand turning circles for large vehicles. They will try to cut

inside you as you start to turn around a blind bend...!

- Beware of cyclists on a descent- those people are crazy!! If you are slow and can safely pull over, let other cars pass and use the right-hand indicator to show your intentions.

What to do if your brakes fail

On our first trip to the Swiss Alps, our brakes failed. It was, without doubt, the most terrified I've ever been on a road trip. Ever.

Here are some tips in case that ever happens to you *touch wood it never does*!

- Try to decelerate as quickly as possible.
- Select a low gear and apply hard pressure to the brake pedal.
- Only pull the handbrake if the road is not slippery (if the surface is wet, you could skid).
- Do NOT put the vehicle into neutral.
- If you can find an emergency road, a run-off road, a field (check there's no ditch) or anywhere safe to run off into, use that.
- Worst case, drive the vehicle sideways into the cliff wall, scraping down the side. It will destroy your vehicle, but you should be slowed to a stop.

Rettungsgasse

Switzerland, German and Austrian law requires drivers to create a Rettungsgasse (emergency vehicle lane)

whenever there is an accident or emergency on the Autobahn. This is so ambulances, police or fire can get to the casualties.
NOTE: This is only for when you are pulling to a stop or very very slow moving.

If there are two lanes (going in the same direction), drivers must move their vehicles to the far right or far left (whichever is closest to you), creating a middle open lane for emergency vehicles. If there are more than two lanes then drivers in the right-side lanes stay far right, while drivers in the middle or left lane(s) go on the far left. The emergency parking lane (hard shoulder) should not be blocked unless signage or a police officer indicates otherwise.
You should keep all doors closed and avoid standing outside the vehicle so you don't get in the way of any emergency service vehicles.

Wildlife accidents

It is a legal requirement to report any accidents involving wildlife to the Police. Around 80% of the country is designated as 'rural', so it is very likely that you may encounter wildlife on your journey. On small roads, be prepared to slow down or stop for cows, goats and sheep.

Security

Switzerland has a low crime rate, but vehicle break-ins do happen, as do petty theft and pickpocketing.

Petrol / Diesel

There are plenty of fuel stations across Switzerland. As with everywhere, you'll find the prices slightly higher on the motorways.

Petrol is Bleifrei (95 / 98), Sans plomb (95 / 98), Senza piombo (95 / 98) - Green handles on pump.

Diesel is called diesel. Black or yellow handles on pump.

Some places are 24h pay at the pump but may require you to go into the shop and pay the cashier either in advance or after you've filled up- there will be a sign to tell you what to do.

You can pay using cash or a credit card. Many places do NOT take American Express. You can usually use your UK cards without a problem.

Getting LPG in Switzerland

LPG (GPL) can be found at selected petrol stations and at autogas stations. If buying from a petrol station, you may need to wait for an attendant to turn the system on for you.

You can find places which sell LPG using MyLPG.eu

Switzerland uses the ACME connector and the Dish connector.

PORTUGAL

Useful things to know

Emergency Numbers: 112 will get you everything
Language: The Portuguese are pretty good at languages. Portuguese is spoken, along with Spanish. Many of the younger generation speak English well.
Currency: Euro
Cards: most major credit and debit cards are accepted. American Express is only taken in large stores (not often at fuel stations).
Time zone: GMT (same as the UK- yes, Spain is one hour ahead).
Mobile Phone and Internet: It's usually possible to use your UK phone and data in Portugal but do check with your provider.
Tipping: Tipping is not expected but appreciated. 5% – 10% in restaurants is standard if you are happy with the service.
Customs: There is no border between Portugal and its EU neighbours.
Shops: Food prices are pretty inexpensive.
Traditionally, shops are open from Monday to Friday, from 9 or 10 a.m. to 7 p.m. Some close for lunch from 1 to 3 p.m. On Saturdays, shops generally close at 1 p.m. though in city centres some are open in the afternoon. Many shops close on Sundays. Bigger supermarkets may be open but will close at lunchtime.

Don't confuse Portugal with Spain; the Portuguese are very proud of their culture and heritage. They enjoy life at a slower pace and there are plenty of queues.

Portugal- why you should go!

Portugal has a little bit of everything- dramatic coastline with sandy beaches, caves, mountains, fantastic cuisine and history. Oh, and wine. Lots and lots of lovely wine. It's wonderfully traditional and many parts of it still feel utterly untouched by the modern world.

One of the best things about being able to explore Portugal on a motorhoming holiday is that you can see the differences between the regions, try the local cuisine (and wine!) and really get a feel for the country in a short space of time. It's also one of the cheapest countries in western Europe, so you can travel on a small budget without much issue.

Where to go and how long for?

If you're driving from the UK to Portugal, you need to allow at least 2 days to get from arriving in France to Portugal. And that's 2 days of pretty much solid driving (it's about 15 and a half hours (1013 miles) from Calais to the north-eastern Portuguese border).

We don't recommend visiting Portugal if you only have a week or your road trip. It's too far and all you'll do is drive there and back. Of course, if you're going to rent a motorhome and fly in, that's perfectly doable in a week.

If you have a couple of weeks, you can certainly explore a good chunk of Portugal. Portugal isn't a huge country, it only takes about 7 hours (470miles) to drive from North to South, so once you're there it's easy to see a lot in a short space of time.

Some of the best places to visit

- The Algarve – the beaches there are some of the best in Europe.
- Lisbon – one of Europe's most historical cities.
- Sintra – it really does look like something from a fairytale.
- Alentejo National Park – the largest protected coastal Natural Park in Europe.
- Porto – one of the oldest ports in the world.
- Cape St Vincent – Europe's most south-westerly point.
- Serra Da Estrela – Portugal's highest mountain range.
- Douro Valley – if you like wine, here's the place to visit.

When to go

Portugal has one of the warmest climates in Europe. As such, it's a magnet for northern Europeans- especially in winter.

Portugal in winter

Portugal is great in winter. It's one of the warmest places in Europe in February with average temperatures of over 16°C. The nice thing about campervanning in Portugal during the winter is that most things remain open, as so many tourists still visit, so it doesn't all shut down like many other countries in Europe. (Of course, some campsites do choose to close, but there are still plenty open all year.)

However, not everywhere in Portugal is warm in winter. Expect snow and skiing in the mountains- especially in Serra Da Estrela (the highest mountain range).

Portugal in summer

For us, summer in Portugal is just too hot. Average temperature in the Algarve in August is 29°C; that's the AVERAGE. As we don't have air conditioning in our motorhome, and because we travel with a dog, we try to avoid hot places like this and go to places with mountains and cooler air.

Also, it gets crowded in summer. Crazy crazy crowded. Beaches are packed and queues for tourist attractions are long. Being crammed in, in hot weather, doesn't appeal to us at all.

Portugal in Spring and Autumn

As with most of Europe, Spring and Autumn are perfect times to explore Portugal. The weather is still warm (average of 19.8°C in April and 22°C in October), but the crowds from summer have gone and you might even get stretches of beach all to yourself.

Driving from the UK to Portugal

If you're planning a trip to Portugal, there are a couple of options from the UK, assuming you're bringing your own vehicle.
There are two ways people get their motorhomes to Portugal: drive through France and Spain or take the ferry to Spain and then drive into Portugal. There are pros and cons to each.

Generally, taking a ferry from the UK is much more expensive than driving through France (depending on the time of year and type of cabin).

Ferry from the UK to Portugal
There are no direct ferries from the UK to Portugal. You can travel with Brittany Ferries from Portsmouth or Plymouth and go to either Santander or Bilbao (both on the north coast of Spain), those are the closest ports to Portugal. Bilbao is about a 5-hour drive from the Portuguese border; around 480km.
A one-way trip on either ferry from the UK takes about 24 hours and booking a cabin is recommended. They also have dog kennels on-board but you CANNOT keep your dog in the ferry cabin with you.

Driving routes through France to Portugal
If you decide that you want to drive your motorhome or camper through France down to Portugal, the quickest

route from Calais is via Le Mans and Bordeaux, crossing into Spain at San Sebastian. Then head towards Valladolid and you're nearly in Portugal.
It takes about 18 hours solid driving from Calais and you can join this route easily if you decide to come over on a ferry to Caen, Le Havre, Dieppe or Cherbourg.

Can I drive to Portugal in the Winter?
Yes. As with Spain, the main routes through the Pyrenees are kept open unless you happen to be unlucky and hit a snowstorm.

If this happens, we recommend stopping for the night somewhere safe and then continuing on when the snow has stopped and the roads have been cleared. Don't forget you will need snow chains and make sure you have fitted all-weather tyres.

Using a Dash-cam in Portugal

This warrants its own section, because so many people don't realise the law. Using a dash-cam in Portugal is illegal. Not just that but OWNING a dash-cam is illegal in Portugal. Leave yours at home.

Things you MIGHT need in Portugal

You will probably want an automatic toll tag, as many of the motorways insist on them before you can use the road. You can avoid these, but it's a lot of extra driving. We use **e-Movis.** Visit their website for more details.

Winter tyres are not compulsory but ARE if driving through France and Spain in winter. Snow chains are mandatory where signage indicates.

Red / white warning board sign, for bike racks or anything overhanging the end of the motorhome or campervan. Lines must point into the middle of the road. This is a legal requirement in Spain, but you'll need it to get to Portugal.

Motorhomes or campers with a total train length of over 12m

If you're travelling in/ through Spain and your outfit exceeds 12m, you need to have marker boards fitted to the back of your vehicle. You can either have two small boards or one large board but they must be placed at the back of the outfit between 50cm and 150cm off the ground.

Your marker board must be yellow in the centre with a red outline, be made out of aluminium and be manufactured to ECE70 standard.

NOTE: This is not law in Portugal, but I fail to see how you're going to get your 12m vehicle train to Portugal without driving through Spain!

Aires in Portugal

There aren't as many aires in Portugal as in France and they're often a little more out of the way, but the network is still very useful and easy to use.

There are a mixture of private and municipal motorhome aires in Portugal. Private aires are very similar to a campsite and often you can stay for as long as you wish.

Municipal aires are approved overnight motorhome stopovers, provided by the local council. At these, there is a restriction of 2-3 nights maximum in one place.

You cannot book motorhome aires in advance as it's first-come, first-served, so if you're visiting at peak times you might feel happier booking a campsite so you're assured of somewhere to stay.

Portugal Easy Camp

Portugal EasyCamp is a scheme which connects local business owners to motorhomers and campervanners looking for safe places to stay overnight.

It works very similarly to France Passion, with one big difference- you have to go online and buy the product or experience BEFORE you visit the location. You can then head there and stay for up to 24 hours.

Wild camping in Portugal

Usually, I am the first person to promote and encourage responsible motorhome wild camping. We enjoy it immensely and have done it across most of Europe with any issues.
Portugal has long been the destination for van owners looking to stay off-grid, despite the fact that wild camping in Portugal has ALWAYS been illegal.

However, the country has been overwhelmed by the sheer numbers of vans in recent years (much like

Scotland) and they have had to deal with years of abuse and mistreatment.
The problem with many of the campervans who visit Portugal is that they don't have their own facilities onboard and people have been leaving waste (of the human kind) all over the place.

On top of that, many wild camping spots don't have any facilities, so people have been leaving piles of rubbish and even emptying their chemical toilets into bushes or over the countryside. Times this by thousands upon thousands of vans and it's no wonder the Portuguese government are trying to protect their country.

Wild camping was never 'legal' in Portugal, but it was tolerated / overlooked if people were considerate and discreet. However, in January 2021, the Portuguese government passed a law which changed the highway code and campervans, motorhomes and caravans had to stay on an official site.

They then changed the law back in summer of 2021… but it's still 'frowned upon' and you're very likely to be moved on.

I'll be honest, I've been appalled by the pictures of waste and vandalism left behind by so many thoughtless and selfish idiots and I can't blame the Portuguese for trying to stop it.

However, there probably aren't enough campsites or Aires to deal with the number of people who visit in vans each year. There will need to be new facilities, more waste and service points and a new infrastructure- and I'm not sure who, when or how it's going to happen.

But there might be a few 'teething problems' for the next couple of years. Either way, I encourage you to avoid wild camping in Portugal as much as possible, even if it is currently 'tolerated' again.

Driving in Portugal

Portuguese drivers have a luke-warm reputation – mainly because the country has one of the highest accident rates in Europe. Having said that, they rarely use indicators and will cut wildly across several lanes to reach an exit. Expect the unexpected and you'll be fine.

Some basic driving rules are:

- Portugal drives on the right.
- Vehicles coming FROM the right have priority at junctions.
- On roundabouts, vehicles already on the roundabout have right of way.
- Seatbelts are compulsory.
- Speeds are in km/h, not mph (you might want to change the setting on your motorhome sat-nav).
- You do not need to have driving lights on during the day.
- Handsfree kits are allowed.
- It is forbidden to use a dash cam or radar detector for speed cameras.

- Road surfaces are generally pretty good in towns and cities but can be bad in the countryside.
- Avoid cities if you're driving in a motorhome, many of them are too crowded and the streets are just not cut out for large vehicles. Park outside and use public transport to get in.
- Trams always have priority everywhere – keep eyes in the back of your head if you're driving near a tram network.
- Emergency vehicles and military vehicles have priority over other road users.
- You may carry a load, such as bikes on a rack, extending by up to 10% of the length of the vehicle to the rear. The load must be indicated by a board/ panel with diagonal red and white stripes- this is legal for Spain, but worth having in Portugal.
- Bikes or a load being carried must NOT be wider than the vehicle.
- Snow chains are mandatory where signage indicates.
- There are no border controls between Spain and Portugal – you can just drive right in..

Roads in Portugal

There has been a lot of money spent in recent years to build new roads (hence all the tolls!) Most of the major roads have been resurfaced and are pretty good, but there are many older roads in more rural areas which are in poorer condition.

You will be fine to drive them with a motorhome or camper but decrease your speed and drive with care.

Traffic Lights in Portugal

Traffic lights use the 3 colour system. There is no amber signal after the red, and a flashing amber light indicates "caution". A flashing or constant red light indicates "stop" and is used near level crossings and to give warning of an obstacle.

Speed Limits in Portugal (unless otherwise signed!)

Breaking the speed limit could result in either an on-the-spot or an automatic fine being sent to you.

Cars and vehicles under 3.5 tonnes:

- 120 km/h (74mph) on motorways and some dual carriageways
- 100km/h (62mph) on major roads
- 90 km/h (56 mph) on minor roads (out of town)
- 50 km/h (31 mph) in built-up areas

Motorhomes and Campervans weighing over 3.5 tonnes:

- motorways 100km/h (62mph)
- major roads 90 km/h (56 mph)
- minor out-of-town roads 80 km/h (50 mph)
- urban areas- 50 km/h (31 mph)

Motorhomes with trailers or caravans

- motorways 100km/h (62mph)
- major out-of-town roads 80 km/h (50 mph)
- minor out-of-town roads 70 km/h (44 mph)
- built-up areas- 50 km/h (31 mph)

Speed Cameras in Portugal

Portugal has many automatic speed cameras and they're quite happy to send tourists a fine through the mail.

You might also find random traffic lights, which turn to red in the middle of nowhere if you're speeding and make you wait for a couple of minutes before turning to green so you can move off again. These are surprisingly effective!

Drink Drive Law in Portugal

Alcohol laws are stricter in Portugal than the UK. The legal limit is 0.05% blood alcohol (the UK is 0.08%) and applies to the driver of any motorised vehicle. If you've had your license for under 3 years, the limit is 0.02%.

A blood alcohol level between 0,5 g/l and 0,8 g/l is considered a serious offence and can cause you to be banned from driving for up to 1 year and a fine of up to 1,250€.

A blood alcohol level between 0,8g/l and 1,2g/l can cause you to be banned from driving for up to 2 years and pay a fine up to 2,500 €

A blood alcohol level of 1,2g/l or more is considered a crime that can be punished with up to 1 year in prison or being banned from driving up to 3 years.

Low Emission zones in Portugal

Portugal does have one low emission zone in Lisbon. About 33% of the city is inside it, so be careful if you drive in.

Tolls in Portugal

There are two types of toll in Portugal- both on motorways:

- traditional motorways with toll booths, where payment is made by cash, bank card or electronic tolls.
- Purely electronic toll motorways. In order to use these roads, you MUST have an electronic device in your vehicle.

Easy Toll

Easy Toll uses your bank card and number plate to take payments. You enter your card details at a sign up location on the border and get a photo of your registration plates taken. The system will then deduct toll payment from your bank card every time your vehicle passes a toll gate.

Signing up costs 0.74€, plus a 0.32€ administrative fee. This method is valid for 30 days, and the tickets issued at the toll must be kept as proof in case of a problem. You can find out more on the Portugal tolls website.

Via Verde

If you regularly use toll roads, it may be worth signing up to the Via Verde scheme which takes you through the fast lane without having to stop and pay.

Via Verde is the only system which works on ALL the Portuguese motorways. It also covers a decent section of Spanish toll roads too. You buy a transponder and then get charged or what you use. The nice thing about them is that once you have one, it doesn't expire, so it's valid for whenever you return to Portugal.

e-Movis

We use e-Movis for tolls all over Europe and we've never had a problem. These allow you to use the VIA-T lanes in Portugal

It's worth noting that you need a DIFFERENT e-Movis tag for Spain and Portugal than you do for France. So if you're driving from the UK to Portugal, you will need at least 2 e-Movis toll tags in your motorhome and you'll need to remember to switch them over (easy to forget-trust me!)

Pre-paid Toll Card

This system is relatively straightforward and handy instructions are written on each card.

You buy a pre-loaded card with either 5, 10, 20 or 40 euros. You then activate the card with an SMS message, using the code printed on the card and the licence plate of the vehicle.

There is a service cost of 0.74 euros for each card purchased.

If you head home with credit still on your toll card you can get this refunded – just return it to the main post office in Portugal, the CTT.

There is also a Toll Service, which is a pre-loaded card with unlimited use for 3 days or previously defined journeys.

You can purchase these at the CTT post office, online at www.tollcard.pt or at various service areas.

Petrol and Diesel

Petrol and diesel are widely available. Many fuel stations are 24h on the main roads and are self-service with card machines.
Petrol is Sem chumbo (95 / 98) - Green handles on pump.
Diesel is Gasóleo or Diesel. Black or yellow handles on pump.
It is not allowed to carry fuel in cans, even in small amounts, so be careful if you have a generator or carry fuel for motorbikes like us.

NOTE: It is illegal to run out of petrol when crossing Lisbon's mile-long 25 de Abril bridge.

LPG Gas

LPG (GPL) can be found at many petrol stations. There are actually more places than in Spain. If buying from a petrol station, you may need to wait for an attendant to turn the system on for you.
You can find places which sell LPG using MyLPG.eu
Portugal mainly uses the euro connector.

Food and Drink in Portugal

Markets are the hub of life in Portugal. You'll find one in every village, town and city, with a range of local produce for sale. Many people in Portugal only eat seasonally, so local dishes will change depending on time of year.

Make sure you have cash (including small change) and bring your own bags. Be warned, the markets are often held in the biggest car park in town, which is often where the motorhome parking is. Pay attention to the signs in these car parks- they will say when the market is and if you are unable to park on certain days.

Local dishes in Portugal to try include:

- pastel de Belém / pastel de nata – DELICIOUS custard tart.
- Francesinha – ham and cheese sandwich.
- Caldeirada de Peixe – stewed fish.
- Salt cod or bacalhau.

Touring Portugal with a dog

Portugal is slowly becoming more dog-friendly. Dogs are now welcome in cafes and restaurants and are allowed on trains- make sure you have a muzzle and their paperwork.

They are not allowed on many beaches in summer and are not allowed into public places like museums. Small dogs in crates are allowed on buses and trams; large dogs are unwelcome on most of them.

IRELAND (Republic and Northern)

The island of 'Ireland' is split into two countries- Northern Ireland (NI, which is part of the UK) and Southern/ Republic of Ireland, which is part of the EU. This has led to all sorts of issues with borders since Brexit and some of the rules are still being ironed out.
Whilst many things are fixed (and we try to update this guide regularly), please do check rules for crossing into Ireland from your country, especially if travelling with a pet as things are still changing.

Useful things to know

Emergency Numbers: 112 or 999 will get you everything
Language: English is the most common language, but Irish Gaelic is common too. Around 18% of the population speak it.
Currency: Euro in Republic, GBP in NI.
Cards: most major credit and debit cards are accepted. American Express is often only taken in large stores (not often at fuel stations)
Time zone: GMT (same as the UK)
Tipping: Tipping 10% in cafes and restaurants is standard if you are happy with the service in either country. A tip for a barman is always appreciated (and can get you access to some hidden whiskies!) Tips for cab drivers and other services are also appreciated.
Shops– Neither Northern Ireland or Southern Ireland are particularly expensive in terms of food or goods- it's about on par with the rest of the UK and you'll see many of the same shops, especially in Northern Ireland. Tesco and Lidl are common.

Southern Ireland is staunchly Catholic, and you may find many shops closed on Sundays and religious days. Some of the larger supermarkets and garages may be open for a few hours. Most shops close between 5pm-7pm during the week- supermarkets may be open as late as 10pm.

Northern Ireland follows the UK, so shops are often open 10-4pm on Sundays and close between 5pm-7pm during the week.

Mobile Phone and Internet: It's usually possible to use your UK phone and data in NI without limits but do check with your provider. In the Republic, it's the same as travelling to any other European country- you'll probably have a data cap (depending on your package.) Just be aware that you could be in Northern Ireland and pick up a Republic of Ireland signal, which might lead to them thinking you're roaming.

Ireland- when to go

Ireland is a beautiful place for a road trip. There's so much history, beautiful roads and locations to explore and plenty of hospitable places to find food and entertainment, both in Northern and Southern Ireland.

Like most of the UK, the best time for a road trip is between April and October due to the weather.

However, remember that it's called the 'Emerald Isle' because it's so green- and it's green because it rains. A lot. Expect rain at any time of the year (yet another reason to be glad of your own vehicle- you can hide inside if the weather turns!)

Of course, there are some sunny days as well, and you're most likely to get those during the summer.

July and August are the main school holidays, so everything will be a lot busier AND prices for everything will be higher- ferries, campsites and even some attraction entrance fees.

There are plenty of major events which happen in Ireland, including the Rugby Six Nations at the beginning of the year (which is mainly centred in Dublin), The Gathering- a traditional dancing and music festival held each February in Kilkenny and St Patrick's Day which is on the 17th March each year- the entire country celebrates with a passion and celebrations often last a week!

There's also the Galway Food Festival in April, motorcycle road races which start in April and May, the Taste of Dublin food festival in June and National Heritage Week at the end of August, as well as many others.
Ireland's winter climate is very similar to the UK's- cold and wet. Snow is not common except in the hills. But this is a much quieter time, and you can experience some crisp sunny days in Autumn and Winter (even if it's not very warm!)

In short, there's never a 'bad' time to visit Ireland. If you're able to travel outside of school holidays, we highly recommend doing that as some places can become incredibly busy.

You can absolutely visit for just a few days - although that can be expensive if you're taking the ferry with a motorhome or campervan. It's much more cost effective to go if you have at least a couple of weeks to explore- we know people who took 10 weeks just to do the Wild Atlantic Way, although you can travel it much faster than that!

Some of the best places to visit in both Northern and Southern Ireland

- Cliffs of Moher - unbelievably dramatic
- The Wild Atlantic Way- 1700 miles of dramatic coastline and traditional Irish culture
- Giants Causeway (Northern Ireland)
- Dark Hedges road- famous as a Game of Thrones filming location. You can drive down it, but not in a motorhome!
- Dublin- one of our favourite cities in Europe
- The Ring of Kerry
- The Rock of Cashel- Ireland's most visited Heritage site
- Blarney Castle and the Blarney Stone
- Dunmore Head- mainland Ireland's most westernmost point
- Torc waterfall

Ireland has also been the location for plenty of movies and TV shows, including:

- Harry Potter and the Half-Blood Prince (Cliffs of Moher, Lemon Rock)
- Star Wars: The Force Awakens/The Last Jedi (Skellig Michael island)
- Braveheart (yes, I know it's about Scotland!)- Bective Abbey, Curragh Plains, Trim Castle)
- Saving Private Ryan Ballinesker Beach- the setting for the D-Day landings in opening 20 minutes
- The Princess Bride (Cliffs of Moher)
- Game of Thrones – all over the place!

Getting from the UK to Ireland with a motorhome or campervan
Before we go any further, let's just go through this again:

- Northern Ireland IS part of the UK. Southern Ireland is not
- Southern Ireland (or the Republic of Ireland) is in the EU. Northern Ireland is not
- Great Britain (or Britain) refers to the landmass of England, Scotland and Wales (NOT Ireland)
- The British Isles is the UK AND Southern Ireland (plus the Channel Islands, Scilly Isles and thousands of other small islands.)

However, even knowing all that, many people (myself included!) incorrectly say going from the UK to Northern Ireland, when they mean from Britain. So, my apologies should I make that error somewhere.
Crossing from Northern Ireland to Southern Ireland
To get to Southern Ireland from Northern Ireland you literally drive across the border.

It used to be incredibly easy- it's now a little harder thanks to BREXIT, but it's still just a matter of driving south. There will be a border to cross and you'll need to carry all the correct documents. There may be a toll charge, depending on your route.

Getting to Ireland by Ferry from rest of the UK

For the rest of the UK (otherwise known as Britain!), if you want to take your own motorhome or campervan across to Ireland, you'll need to get on a ferry.

There are a few ferry routes to choose from:

- Holyhead to Dublin (Irish Ferries)
- Pembroke to Rosslare (Irish Ferries)
- Liverpool to Dublin (P&O Ferries)
- Cairnryan to Larne (P&O Ferries)
- Cairnryan to Belfast (Stena Line)
- Liverpool to Belfast (Stena Line)
- Holyhead to Dublin (Stena Line)
- Fishguard to Rosslare (Stena Line)

Getting to Ireland from France

There are also ferries which go directly from France to Ireland. Not all of these are daily- some are only once a week or so.

- Cherbourg to Dublin (Irish Ferries)
- Cherbourg to Rosslare (Brittany Ferries)
- Roscoff to Cork (Brittany Ferries)
- Roscoff to Rosslare (Brittany Ferries)
- Cherbourg to Rosslare which runs three times a week (Stena Line)

Travelling around Ireland

Once you're over in Ireland, whether it's North or South, the road system is very good and easy to navigate. We'll talk more about the rules, speed limits and other things to know shortly.

Hiring a motorhome to tour Ireland

Of course, if you don't have or want to pay to take your vehicle to Ireland, or you're travelling from further away, the easiest option is to fly in to Ireland and rent a motorhome or campervan to use during your stay. Just make sure to ask how to get from the airport to the rental agency- not all of them are at the airport itself and you might need to book a taxi.

The biggest airports in Ireland are:
Dublin Airport – east coast
Cork Airport – south coast
Shannon Airport – west coast (near Limerick)
Knock Airport – mid/ north West (but still in Southern Ireland)
Belfast Airport – in Northern Ireland

Things you need to carry to legally drive in Ireland

You'll be pleased to know that Ireland is similar to the rules in the UK, so there are very few things you LEGALLY have to carry (although we recommend them anyway.) These are:

- UK Sticker attached to the back of vehicle or reg plates (and trailer if you have one)
- A spare wheel (and tools to change it!), or a tyre repair kit.
- If you wear glasses you MUST carry a spare pair
- Crash helmets are mandatory for motorbike/ moped riders and passengers

NOTE: Hi-vis reflective jackets and headlight beam (if you have a UK vehicle) are not required in Ireland. If you have a European vehicle (ie- you normally drive on the right), you will need headlight converters.

Motorhome Stopovers and Overnight camper parking in Ireland

Like most countries in Europe, there are several types of places where you can stop with your motorhome or campervan overnight in Ireland.

- Campsites
- Free/ approved motorhome parking schemes

- Wild Camping (we'll talk more about the legality of that shortly)

Motorhome Campsites in Ireland
Campsites in Ireland are much like other campsites anywhere around the UK or Europe. Some have pools, entertainment and more, while others are more basic (and usually cheaper!)

You normally don't need to book sites up in advance unless you're visiting in peak season or during a festival (or over St Patrick's weekend.
Be aware that many campsites close for winter, some as early as September and don't re-open until Easter. So do your research, especially if you're travelling out of season.

Aires in Ireland

Ireland, like the UK, does not have a system of 'aires' in the same way you might be used to in France, Germany or Italy.
An aire is just an approved overnight motorhome parking area which isn't a campsite. Ireland DOES have many places where motorhomes and campervans can stay overnight- with permission. But they don't work in the same way as aires.

Approved overnight motorhome parking

There are several schemes which connect motorhomers and campervanners who don't want to stay in campsites every night to businesses and places happy to allow overnight parking (usually without facilities). This is in exchange for you buying some of their products or services, such as a meal in a restaurant.
One such scheme is Safe Nights Ireland– which has over 350 locations around Northern and Southern Ireland. You

can join the scheme for just 15€ a year and get access to any places which are part of the scheme.

Pub Overnight Stops in Ireland

Pubs are a great option for a free overnight parking stop if you're already going to eat at them. Many of them will allow motorhomes and campervans to stay overnight in their car parks (some even allow caravans). Obviously, this is only for the night- you probably wouldn't be able to stay there for a week, although I suppose there's no harm in asking!

Wild parking in Ireland

By the letter of the law, you're not allowed to stay anywhere with a motorised vehicle apart from on approved campsites, unless you have the landowner's permission.

However many people do motorhome wild parkups all over Ireland and rarely have a problem.

Don't forget, overnight parking is parking up for one night and then moving on again in the morning. No awnings, outdoor furniture, BBQs, generators, washing lines or anything OUTSIDE the vehicle.
In many remote places, if you arrive late in the afternoon and leave early-ish in the morning, you'll be absolutely fine to stay overnight, unless there's a clear sign banning motorhomes or campers overnight.
Remember, you can always ask if you're allowed to stay. The Irish are incredibly hospitable and if you're polite and respectful, they're very likely to allow you to stay without

issue (especially if you've just paid money to them for something!)

Motorhome and campervan service points in Ireland
Unlike on mainland Europe, there are very few places to discharge waste and water and refill with fresh water apart from on the campsites. For this reason, it's worth booking into a campsite for a night every few days, in order to use its services.

Driving tips for Ireland

Ireland has a fairly good road network, especially around the major towns and cities. However, some of the smaller rural roads can be VERY narrow and many are marked as unsuitable for larger vehicles, like motorhomes.

Often, these small roads are single track, and have passing places. These are places to pull in to let another vehicle go past from the other direction, NOT somewhere to park up and go for a walk.
Also, expect slow-moving farm vehicles on these roads- it can take a while to get anywhere and no-one in Ireland is in much of a hurry. So don't over-estimate how far you can travel in one day. Also, expect sheep, cows and other animals to wander out into the road in front of you at any moment.

- Drive on the left (like in the UK, the opposite to most of Europe)
- Stay to the left on roads with more than one lane and overtake on the right.
- At roundabouts and junctions, traffic already on the road and coming from the right has priority.
- Motorways are marked with an 'M'

- Seatbelts are compulsory for front and rear passengers
- All children up to 135 cms in height or up to 12 years of age, must use a suitable child seat (Northern Ireland)
- Handsfree kits are required if using a mobile phone
- Devices warning of speed cameras are forbidden
- Dipped headlights are to be used during poor visibility.
- Motorcycles must use dipped headlights during the day at all times.

Speed Limits in Ireland

IMPORTANT: Southern Ireland drives in km/h (like most of Europe). Northern Ireland drives in mph (like the rest of the UK). If you change the settings on your sat nav, remember to change it if you cross the border!

Breaking the speed limit in either Northern or Southern Ireland will result in a fixed penalty and/ or penalty points on your driving licence.
On the spot fines are rare, but it is possible to be pulled over by the police force for speeding and given a fixed penalty notice and/ or plus a £100 fine.

SOUTHERN IRELAND

Speed Limits for vehicles under 3.5t are as follows (unless otherwise signed!)

- Motorways- 120km/h (74mph)
- National roads/ dual carriageways- 100 km/h (62 mph)
- Regional roads- 80km/h (50mph)
- Built up areas- 50 km/h (31 mph)
-

Speed limits for vehicle OVER 3.5t

- Motorways/ – 90 km/h (55 mph)
- National roads/ dual carriageways- 80 km/h (50 mph)
- Regional roads- 80km/h (50mph)
- Built up areas- 50 km/h (31 mph)
-

Speed limits in Northern Ireland

- Motorways/ – 70 mph
- National roads/ dual carriageways- 60mph
- Built up areas- 30 mph (50kph)

Speed cameras in Ireland

There are both static and mobile speed cameras in Ireland. The mobile ones are mostly in vans which are moved around as the Irish police force (Garda Síochána) see fit.

Drink driving laws

Southern Ireland has stricter drink driving laws than Northern Ireland, only allowing 50 milligrammes of alcohol in 100 millilitres of blood (the UK and Northern Ireland is 80). As always, don't drink and drive. If you are a new or a professional driver, the levels are even lower.

Tolls in Ireland

There are currently no toll roads in Northern Ireland.
There are 11 toll roads in Southern Ireland- not as many as you might be used to in France or Norway! You can see where they are on the etoll.ie website.
You can pay for the tolls using cash at the toll plazas (cards are accepted at a few but not all). Alternatively, you can sign up for a TollTag account and that will charge you as you drive.

The only road where you cannot pay as you drive is the M50. The M50 works a bit like a Dartford Tunnel- you need to pay for using it by 8pm the following day. You can pay at many garages and shops in the area, but the easiest way is online at eflow.ie

If you are renting a vehicle, you will need to ask them how to pay for tolls/ the M50 but it's common for you to need to pay yourself.

Petrol/ Diesel in Ireland

There are plenty of fuel stations across Ireland. As with everywhere, you'll find the prices slightly higher on the motorways.

Petrol is Unleaded (95 / 98) – Green handles on pump
Diesel has black or yellow handles on pump
Some places are 24h pay at the pump, but may require you to go into the shop and pay the cashier either in advance or after you've filled up- there will be a sign to tell you what to do. (Leave your car in front of the pump and make a note of the pump number.)

You can pay using cash or a credit card. Many places do NOT take American Express. You can use your UK cards without a problem.

Parking in Ireland

Many places which allow parking during the day or night require payment. Usually, you need to pay at the ticket machine display your parking ticket in the windscreen. Not doing this is likely to result in a fine.
Parking is **prohibited** when the road is marked with a red line or a double yellow line.

A disadvantage of a campervan in Ireland is that parking in cities and towns can be tough- many places have height barriers of around 2.5m (and most vans and motorhomes are taller than that!) Therefore, you would need to find on-street parking in the town, which can be difficult. Alternatively, park up or use a campsite nearby and use public transport to get in.

Getting LPG in Ireland

LPG (GPL) can be found at selected petrol stations and at autogas stations. If buying from a petrol station, you may need to wait for an attendant to turn the system on for you.

Getting to Ireland from Britain with a dog

Now that BREXIT has been and gone, the rules for entering Ireland with a dog have changed.
In order for your dog to travel into Ireland, you will need:

- A Microchip
- A rabies vaccination (you must wait 21 days before travel)
- An Animal Health Certificate (or Pet Passport for European pets)
- A Tapeworm treatment, administered 1-5 days before travel by an approved vet. (Note: you do NOT need tapeworm for going from Ireland to Britain)

The rules for travelling with a pet between Northern and Southern Ireland are still being discussed and could well change within the next few years. For the most up-to-date information, check the Deara website.

Congratulations!

Whoop! You made it to the end (apart from the Appendices, but close enough!)
As I've said several times already, there is a LOT of information here. Please don't feel overwhelmed if you don't remember it all; the beauty of this guide is you can return to it again and again whenever you need to and of course you can take it with you on your travels.

My main aim is for you to feel much more confident and knowledgeable about what to expect when you travel to Europe.
It's absolutely impossible for me to show you every scenario you might encounter during your Europe trip, but I hope I've answered as many of your questions as possible.

Don't forget, if you need to buy any kit, want to see what we use or want to grab any of the checklists in a printable format, just scan here >>>
or head to: https://wandering-bird.com/europe-travel-resource-page

Now, all that remains is for me to say "you got this!" I know it can be intimidating, but the rewards far outweigh the fear once you get going, I promise.

I'd love to know where you end up- feel free to tag us on Instagram or Facebook (details below)

Have an amazing adventure and safe travels.

Kat x

Come chat with me on:

Instagram: @wanderingbird.adventures

Facebook: wanderingbird.adventures

Our Wandering Bird Motorhoming Facebook group

About the Author

Kathryn Bird is an ex-air traffic controller who decided to get out of the rat race whilst she was still young enough to enjoy it.
She quit her job and now explores Europe by motorhome and motorbike, sharing her experiences on the award-winning travel blog **Wandering Bird**.

She is passionate about inspiring others to have their own adventures and experience the freedom of life on the road, whether it's a long weekend or a month away.

You can read more about Kathryn's adventures, tips and 'How to' guides at **www.wandering-bird.com** where you can also find checklists, itinerary ideas and guides to help you have your own epic adventures in your van.

Next Steps

If you'd like more guidance, including:

- Setting up your motorhome
- Wild camping with a van
- In-depth guides on France, Scotland or Wales travel

you can find them all here >>>

SCAN ME

(use code **THANKS10** to get 10% off everything)

We also designed an exclusive Road Trip logbook for you to use and record your adventures. Find it at the link above- it's a wonderful way to capture memories and look back at them for years to come.

Appendices

Gear Packing List

You can see all the essentials we recommend you carry, including the kit we use, **here >>>**

You can also grab your free printable packing checklist from there too

Essentials Every Van Needs

- Hosepipe (10-15m)
- Hoselock & brass connectors – ½", ¾" & 1" threads to cover most taps
- Collapsible water carrier/ watering can
- Funnel
- Collapsible bucket
- Electric cable (25m)
- Splitter cable
- European adapter
- 230v wall plug for Europe (see post above for more details)
- Gas bottles OR refillable adapters- take spanner for exchangeable bottles
- Levelling chocks

- Mud mats
- Fire blanket
- Fire extinguisher
- Smoke & CO alarm
- Window vacuum (we love Karcher)
- Toilet chemicals & paper
- Grey waste tank cleaner
- Spare bulbs
- Warning Triangle
- Tyre inflater/ repair kit
- Wing mirror protectors
- Cleaning supplies

Kitchen basics

- Plates / bowls
- Cutlery
- Glasses
- Mugs
- Pans/ saucepan
- Wooden stirrer
- Spatula
- Bottle opener & corkscrew
- Tin opener
- Slotted spoon
- Sharp knives
- Water jug
- Storage boxes for food
- Chopping boards
- Cheese grater

- Measuring jug
- Weighing scales
- Scissors (2 pairs)
- Peeler
- Masher
- Wooden skewers
- Tea towels
- Washing up gear
- Cleaning wipes
- Pan protectors and non-slip matting to stop rattles
- Sink plug
- Plunger
- Dustpan & brush (we have a mini one)
- 12v vacuum cleaner
- Kitchen roll
- Tin foil
- Cling film

Bedroom Basics

- Duvet or sleeping bag
- Pillows
- Bedding
- Spare Bedding
- Mattress Topper if using
- Blanket
- Laundry bag
- Laundry detergent & softener
- Clothes Pegs

Outdoor living

- Table
- Folding chairs
- BBQ & tools
- Matches / lighter
- Picnic rug
- Citronella candles/ spray
- Outdoor lights
- Awning
- Outdoor blanket

Clothes & Personal Lists

As I type this, I am surrounded by piles of clothes, getting ready for another adventure.
I figure if I list what I'm planning to take with us for a 2 month Europe tour, you can scale accordingly for your road trip.
In no particular order... it's boiling hot as I write this so beach stuff is on my mind!! ☺

- Swimming costume / Bikini
- Goggles
- If you're going somewhere beachy, a lightweight coverup for the beach which protects arms/ shoulders if it get too hot.
- Sunhat
- Scarf / shawl

- Fluffy socks (in place of slippers!)
- Pyjamas
- Tights (I wear these under my bike gear)
- Knee support
- Sports Kit (see above) to include bra, socks, leggings, t-shirts.
- Underwear
- Socks
- Shorts 2/3 pairs
- Skirts (1 long, 1 short)
- Dresses 1/2
- Jeans 2/3
- Combats / lightweight trousers
- Joggers (For lounging, not exercise!)
- T-shirts- 3/4
- Vest Tops 4/5
- Hoody x 2
- Cardigan/ jumper x 2
- Fleece
- Warm hat / scarf / gloves
- Waterproof jacket (ideally one with fleece or layers).
- Jewellery if you're bringing it. (Bring small bag to put it in if going to beach).
- Sunglasses
- Walking shoes/ boots
- Cheap sandals for wearing at beach/ lake which might get wet.
- Nice shoes for meal out.
- Trainers

- Lightweight coat with hood

Campervan Essential Kit- Toiletries

- Shampoo
- Conditioner
- Body wash
- Shaving kit
- Toothbrushes
- Toothpaste
- Mouthwash
- Deodorant
- Body Spray
- Face cream with SPF
- Face / body wipes
- Night cream
- Eye cream
- Suntan lotion
- 50 strength suntan lotion
- Aftersun
- Body lotion
- Antiseptic hand wash
- Leave in hair conditioning spray (Awesome for warm climates).
- Hairbrush
- Hair bands
- Cotton buds
- Cotton pads
- Perfume
- Contacts

- Medicine (including Contraception)
- Sanitary Protection
- Hairdryer
- Dry shampoo
- Tweezers
- Nail clippers
- Glasses / contact lenses / contact solution
- SPARE GLASSES – legal requirement

Make up

- Foundation / tinted moisturiser
- Sponge
- Concealer
- Eye shadow
- Blush
- Eye liner
- Mascara
- Lip balm
- Lip stick
- Nail varnish / remover

Medication

- Antiseptic (we have individual wipes and a tube of Savlon).
- Painkillers (Nurofen & paracetamol)
- Wound-cleaning gauze
- Plasters of various sizes
- Spray plaster
- Tweezers
- Nail clippers

- Thermometer
- Child-friendly medicines, like Calpol
- Bonjela for mouth ulcers
- Antihistamines / hayfever tablets
- Suntan lotion (include different strengths as required).
- Aftersun treatment
- Voltarol or similar for pain relief
- Deep heat spray (miracle worker!)
- Insect repellent spray
- Insect bite treatment
- Safety pins
- Eye-wash kit
- Anti-blister kits or stuff to put in shoes which are rubbing- so useful if you're doing a lot of hiking.
- Medication for pre-existing medical conditions.
- Cough medicine
- Vaporub
- Antiseptic throat spray / lozenges
- Imodium
- Windeze
- Sudafed

First Aid Kit

- 6 x wound dressings (10cm x 10cm)
- 2 x triangular badges (136cm x 96cm x 96 cm)
- 2 x first aid dressings (40cm x 60cm)

- 1 x first aid dressing (60cm x 80cm)
- 3 x first aid compress (8cm x 10cm)
- 2 x bandages (4m x 6cm)
- 3 x bandages (4m x 8cm)
- 1 x emergency blanket (160cm x 210cm)
- 8 x adhesive plasters (10cm x 6cm)
- 1 x pair of scissors
- 1 x adhesive tape (5m x 2.5cm)

Other Personal Items

- Towels
- Face cloths
- Beach towels / rugs for sitting on
- Cards
- Headphones
- Speaker
- Portable Charger
- Hard-drive
- Wi-Fi Dongle
- USB charger
- Wallet
- Small Bag
- Beach bag / backpack
- Kindle or books
- Beach games / football / Boules
- Electronic games
- Portable DVD player / iPad (if downloading games/ video – try to do it before you leave).

- Torch
- Spare batteries
- Ear plugs

Don't forget, you can get printable checklists, road trip planning sheets, maintenance checklists and much more at www.wandering-bird.com

Scan here to visit >>>

Safe travels!

Kat x

Printed in Great Britain
by Amazon